Christo

# Remaking

# a broken

# world

## The heart of the Bible story

Remaking a Broken World
This revised edition © Christopher Ash / The Good Book Company, 2019

Previously published by Authentic Media, 2010

Published by:
The Good Book Company

thegoodbook.com | www.thegoodbook.co.uk
thegoodbook.com.au | thegoodbook.co.nz | thegoodbook.co.in

ISBN: 9781784983765 | Printed in the UK

Design by André Parker

# CONTENTS

Introduction: Beginning With the God Who is One    7

Section A – A Broken World:
Scattered Without God    21
   1. Eden: Expelled to Wander    25
   2. Babel: Scattered by Pride    39

Section B – The Assembly of Israel:
Gathering Foreshadowed    59
   3. Sinai: Gathered Under the Word    61
   4. Jerusalem: Gathered Under the King    87
   5. Babylon: Back to Babel    107

Section C – The Assembly of Jesus:
Gathering Realized    129
   6. Golgotha: Gathered to Jesus    131
   7. Pentecost: Gathered by the Spirit    147
   8. Church: Gathered Worldwide    163

Section D – The New Creation:
Gathering Consummated    195
   9. The New Creation: Gathered Forever    197

Conclusion: The Glory of the God Who is One    219

Endnotes    221
Index of Biblical References    225
Acknowledgements    235

*To Emmanuel, Wimbledon*

# SUMMARY DIAGRAM

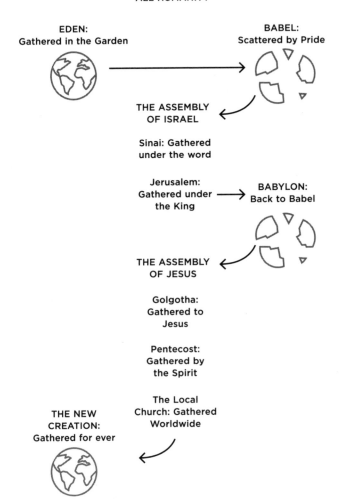

ALL HUMANITY

**EDEN:**
Gathered in the Garden

**BABEL:**
Scattered by Pride

**THE ASSEMBLY
OF ISRAEL**

Sinai: Gathered
under the word

Jerusalem:
Gathered under
the King

**BABYLON:**
Back to Babel

**THE ASSEMBLY
OF JESUS**

Golgotha:
Gathered to
Jesus

Pentecost:
Gathered by
the Spirit

The Local
Church: Gathered
Worldwide

**THE NEW
CREATION:**
Gathered for ever

# Beginning With the God Who is One

### How is a Broken World to be Remade?

We live in a world that is fractured on every level. From the family to international relations, it is hard to make and maintain harmony. Every day the news brings stories of broken relationships, strife-ridden communities and warring nations. How can it be restored to peace?

The thesis of this little book is that the ordinary local Christian church contains within itself the seeds, or the DNA, of a remade world. That will seem a very surprising thesis to those who think the local church is a complete irrelevance to the real world; and it will be greeted with ironic smiles by those whose experience of local churches is one of strife and tension. But I believe it to be true.

I want to persuade us to commit ourselves wholeheartedly to belonging to, and serving God in the fellowship of, a local church; and that this may prove to be the most significant thing we do with our lives. I want to convince us that the local church is at the heart of the Bible story, that it is close to the heart of the purposes of God, and that it is how a broken world will be remade. I want you to share my passion that the glory of God is inseparably tied up with what happens in the local church.

This message is important in a culture of choice where we are used to being able to shop around for what we want. A survey of attitudes amongst non-churchgoers included a positive take on "spirituality" side by side with a negative attitude to religion. This was compared by one young man to the difference between playing football and being a member of a football team. He was happy with "spirituality" as a means of fulfilling his personal ambitions (like kicking around a football) but very unhappy at the idea of being constrained by being a committed member of a community (like belonging to a football team). Another commented, "If I am going to believe in something I will pick my favourite parts of different religions or pick something that I have invented … that I feel comfortable with … Not what I'm expected to believe in"; another said, "We take a little bit from this belief and a bit from that, and a bit from the other and then we come to our own major conclusion to live our lives by."[1] It's all a matter of what I choose.

These personal choice, pick'n'mix attitudes get translated when people become Christians, and they then appear amongst Christians in slightly different clothes. Christians can easily slip into church shopping (finding a church that meets our needs) and church hopping (moving around from church to church without settling into any one). We can get the idea that the Christian life is about special big events and celebrity speakers and find ourselves picky spectators, more interested in evaluating the church experiences on offer than in the hard graft of building deep relationships together shaped by the word of God.

## What's the Point of A(nother) Bible Overview?

I want to persuade you, by a grand sweep through the whole Bible, that to belong in a committed and relational way to an ordinary local church may be the most significant thing you do with your life. I am going to try to do that from the whole Bible. That is to say, this book is an overview of the whole Bible story, a shortened and simplified version, an attempt to sum up the Bible story in brief. I used to live a short bike ride from the British Museum in the heart of London. Sometimes on a day off my wife and I cycled up there for a visit. The British Museum is a huge and fascinating place: it is hard to know where to start. So, in their wisdom, the people who run it offer a "One Hour Tour" of the museum. They show you some of the highlights, such as the Rosetta Stone and the Parthenon marbles. You can't really begin to see the museum in one hour. But, by taking you round some of the highlights, they hope to whet your appetite to return again and again to explore the treasures.

A Bible overview is a way in to reading the Bible, not a way round. It is like a series of signposts to help us reach a city centre rather than a bypass to make it unnecessary for us to go to the city centre at all. The Bible is greater than the sum of its overviews. You may be familiar perhaps with one overview; I hope you are, because many people have found a Bible overview a helpful way to start finding their way around the Bible. It can give us a sense of how it fits together.

My favourite first overview is *God's Big Picture*, by Vaughan Roberts; this is themed around how the Bible tells the story of the kingdom of God.[2] I have also been greatly helped and stimulated by T. Desmond Alexander's overview, *From Eden to the New Jerusalem*.[3] But because overviews have to choose some governing theme, they all need to omit parts of the Bible that don't tie very closely to that theme. Every Bible overview omits more than it includes. Overviews are like different types of map. One map may highlight physical characteristics such as contours; another may give you the transport networks; a third may focus on political boundaries; a fourth on population density. Each is of value. But the reality of visiting the place will always be greater than the sum of all the maps you can lay your hands on.

## Scattering and Gathering

So here's the reason I'm offering you an alternative Bible overview: I want to show you a fresh camera angle on the Bible story, one that brings the local church into sharp focus.

I'm going to tell the Bible story in a way that highlights scattering and gathering: scattering as a sign of God's judgment and gathering as a sign of God's rescue. To do that, I will of course miss out a very great deal. Maybe you have seen a photo of a familiar place, but taken from an unfamiliar camera angle or taken with a different kind of lens (perhaps a wide-angle lens rather than a telephoto lens). Perhaps you find yourself looking at a photo of a street you may have known from childhood, and yet noticing things that you have never seen before. No one camera angle or lens will encapsulate the whole experience of living in the street: but they may open our eyes to significant things we had not seen before.

A few years ago my wife and I decided to try to learn about wild flowers near the coast in South Wales where we were on holiday. Armed with our pocket guide to wild flowers, we set out. Before long, we spotted our first Viper's Bugloss. But having spotted one, it wasn't long before we were seeing these lovely little wild flowers all over the place. I am so unobservant I had never seen them before at all, though I must have walked by hundreds of them. My hope is that this distinctive Bible overview will open our eyes to the significance of the local church.

Incidentally, this camera angle is not necessarily any better or worse than other camera angles. People sometimes ask how we can know whether a particular Bible overview is "the right one". The answer is: they all are and none of them is, though some are more valuable than others. Imagine a photographer taking a photograph of a great sculpture for an illustrated book. No camera angle would be wrong, but some might show off the sculpture better than others. The test is whether or not a photo gives readers a good two-dimensional "feel" for the majesty of the three-dimensional statue. You will have to judge to what extent the scattering and gathering theme gives us an overall grasp of the Bible story.

## Beginning with the God Who is One

Let us start with God. A famous Christian of the fourth century wrote that, "the very best order of ... every speech and action, is to begin from God and to end in God".[4] He was right: we shall start and end our story with God.

### The Lord our God, the Lord is One

Our starting text is one of the most famous verses in the Bible:

Hear, O Israel: The LORD our God, the LORD is one
(Deuteronomy 6 v 4)

This is the famous "Shema" recited regularly in synagogues for centuries ("Shema" is the Hebrew word for "Hear!" or "Listen!"). Moses is preaching to the people of God just before they moved into the Promised Land. There are just four Hebrew words in the statement he makes: The-LORD our-God the-LORD One (In Hebrew, "the LORD" is one word, as is "our God").

11

"The Lᴏʀᴅ" in capital letters in our English translations is sometimes written "Yahweh" or "Jehovah"; it is the Hebrew name of the God of the Bible. He is the God of Abraham, Isaac, and Jacob, the God of Moses and of the Exodus. He is the God who makes a covenant (or agreement) with his people. The strapline of the covenant is, "You will be my people and I will be your God" (e.g. Exodus 6 v 7 or Ezekiel 36 v 28). Moses calls him "our God", not because he is the private god of Israel (as if there were lots of other valid gods and goddesses) but because he is the God who is in covenant relationship with Israel.

The emphasis and climax of the statement is the word "one": the God of the Bible story, the covenant God in relationship with us, is *one*! This is a huge statement; it is rather like a part of a website that is full of hyperlinks elsewhere; it connects all over the Bible story. This is not a simple mathematical oneness that would stop God being Father, Son and Holy Spirit, one God in Trinity, as we shall see in Chapter 7 (e.g. 1 Corinthians 8 v 6). So what does it mean?

*1. One God*

First, it means that the God of the Bible is the only real God. Centuries later the apostle Paul wrote to the church in Corinth, "We know that 'An idol is nothing at all in the world' and that 'There is no God but one.'" (1 Corinthians 8 v 4). The words "is nothing at all in the world" mean that an idol "has no real existence" (ESV). Of course, a god or goddess such as a Hindu god or the Muslim Allah exists, in a sense; but they exist only in the imaginations of their worshippers. They do not have any substantial, objective existence independent of the minds and hearts of their worshippers. If their worshippers ceased to worship them, they would cease to exist. Only the God of the Bible exists independently of us: we could cease to exist and yet he would still exist. His divinity and reality would be unaffected.

## 2. One reality

Second, this verse therefore means that there is only one objective and substantial reality in the universe. This may sound rather philosophical, but it is important. I remember listening to a young woman called Julia telling her story. Julia had been brought up in a Christian home and had then gone to study Geography at university. There she had been immersed in a worldview in which it was firmly and repeatedly asserted that there is "no one reality". There is "my reality" and there is "your reality". "Your reality" may be real and true in a subjective sense "for you"; and yet "my reality" (which may contradict "your reality") can still be true or real "for me". In the intellectual world where Julia studied it was insisted upon (yes, really insisted upon, as if *this* truth were somehow really true!) that there is no one reality that is real in the whole world.

This is a world many of us inhabit at school or university or in the workplace. Not surprisingly Julia said she became confused, because a world with no one reality is a very confusing place. It was not until she found her rest in the one real God that her confusion was replaced by clarity. One true God means that there is one objective substantial reality within which you and I have to live. We can create our subjective or virtual quasi-realities as much as we like, but the day will come when we must reckon with what one theologian called "the God who is there", and therefore with the reality that is there.[5]

## 3. One morality

Third, a consequence of this is that there is one objective morality: there is such a thing as right and such a thing as wrong; morality is objectively true and not subjectively relative. By and large our culture does not accept this. The writer Will Self described the cultural world of his childhood like this: he was brought up in "a world where ethics, so far from inhering in the very structure of the cosmos, was a matter of personal taste akin to a designer label, sewn into the inside lining of conscience".[6] It is a vivid image: you choose your ethics label, and I choose mine, but it is no more than a matter of personal taste.

Taken to its logical conclusion, this is a frightening world, in which a paedophile or serial killer can claim that they are following their own personal moral code, and who are we to say they are objectively wrong? However, in the poetic language of the Old Testament, the world is not like a chaotic sea, with right and wrong shifting wildly from side to side in the waves. Instead it is firmly placed on pillars or foundations, a secure moral order rooted in the reality of the God who is One. For example, when Hannah the mother of the prophet Samuel celebrates the justice of God she sings, "For the *foundations* of the earth are the LORD's; on them he has set the world" (1 Samuel 2 v 8). That is, in Will Self's words, right and wrong do inhere "in the very structure of the cosmos."

## 4. Harmony under one ruler
Finally, all this means that there ought to be universal harmony under one ruler. The world is a coherent place because it is made and sustained by one real God. It is not the playground or battlefield of many gods and goddesses all competing for supremacy, vying for the superior places in the heavenly Cabinet chamber. This is very different from the world of animism, in which we are at the mercy of the spirits of trees, of rivers, and of mountain tops. It is very different from the world of the Greek and Roman pantheons which formed the

culture of the New Testament world around the Mediterranean Sea. It is very different from the thousands of Hindu gods and goddesses. The world is not like Iraq after the toppling of Saddam Hussein, a country riven with competing people groups, or the Balkans after Marshal Tito, disintegrating into warring regions like Bosnia, Serbia, Kosovo and Croatia. Nor is it like an anarchic school playground where the teachers are absent and life is one long fight for survival and supremacy.

*The Bible story in three acts*
But here's the problem: the world quite clearly is not living in harmony under one ruler. It is all too much like an anarchic playground. The Bible recognises precisely this tension. The clearest echo of the Shema in the Old Testament comes right near the end of Israel's history before Christ. After the exile in Babylon, the prophet Zechariah looks forward to a future day when "the LORD will be king over all the earth. On that day the LORD will be one and his name one" (Zechariah 14 v 9 ESV).[7]

In many places the Bible asserts that God is already king over all the earth. For example, he is "the LORD Most High … the great King over all the earth" (Psalm 47 v 2). So how can Zechariah look forward to a future day when he "*will be* king over all the earth" if he is already king? Or, to put it another way, how can the Bible assert so firmly that the LORD is one and at the same time look forward to a day when the LORD will be one (Deuteronomy 6 v 4; Zechariah 14 v 9)? I think the answer is in the parallel statement in Zechariah: "and his *name* one". His "name" speaks not just of his identity but also of his reputation, of human beings acknowledging his kingship. In one sense, he is king over the whole earth now but, in another sense, he isn't. In one sense, he is "one" now but, in another sense, he isn't. He is king in the sense that he governs the world exactly as he pleases: he is the Sovereign Lord. And he is "one" in the sense that his reality and glory undergird creation. But he is not universally acknowledged ("named") and known as the one true God. His world is peopled by rebels who are governed by God despite their hostility and against their will. Zechariah looks forward to that great day when the renewed creation will be governed by God through a redeemed humanity who will gladly bow the knee and praise him. But we are jumping ahead to the end of the story.

The story of the Bible is the story of how God will bring about that great day. The Bible may be thought of as a story in three acts. Act I is very brief, because it lasts only until Genesis 3. We might call Act I "Harmony". God makes one coherent creation, a universe in which his will is done perfectly and without complexity equally in "heaven" (God's space) and on "earth" (our space-time universe); there is no curtain or barrier between God's space ("heaven") and our space ("earth").

Act II may be called "Fracture", and it lasts from Genesis 3 until near the end of the book of Revelation. In Act II, although God continues to be the sovereign ruler of the universe, his will is not done on "earth" in the same way as it is done in "heaven" (which is why we must pray in the Lord's Prayer, "Your will be done, on earth as it is in heaven", Matthew 6 v 10). Now it is a case of, "God is in heaven and you are on earth, so let your words be few" (Ecclesiastes 5 v 2). Because human beings break away from God's loving rule and decide to live their lives without reference to the God who made them, the whole universe is put out of joint, and humanity becomes fractured and scattered. Fault lines appear all over the place, and men and women are at war with one another and misgoverning a world that cries out to be well-governed.

The world is a broken place because it is alienated from the God who made it.

And yet the God who made it has not given up on it. He is at work to remake the world he still loves. God is determined not to be defeated. He will win, and his victory will see his world remade as he intended it to be. This is why Act III is "The New Creation", the new heavens and new earth (i.e. the renewed and restored universe), which is pictured for us in apocalyptic language at the end of the book of Revelation.

However, a Bible overview that simply divided the Bible storyline into three parts like this would not be very helpful to Bible readers. It would put less than 1 per cent into Act I and Act III and leave over 99 per cent of the Bible in Act II! So I am going to shape our tour around nine critical Bible places or events on the way.

### The Bible story in nine places

Our Bible tour is going to start in Eden, and then pause at Babel, Sinai, Jerusalem, Babylon, Golgotha, Pentecost, and Church, before concluding in the New Creation.

We are going to begin in the garden in Eden, with harmony, the nucleus of a gathered humanity close to God. We shall see that harmony tragically broken, and pause at the iconic story of the Tower of Babel in Genesis 11 to see the fractured world vividly pictured for us. The movement from Eden to Babel speaks of a world that is scattered and fractured because it is alienated from the creator God who is One.

From Babel we will fast-forward through the promises God made to Abraham, Isaac, and Jacob, and the great rescue of God's people from Egypt (the Exodus), to Mount Sinai where the Ten Commandments and the Law of Moses were given. At Sinai the people of God assemble by the mountain under God's spoken word of law: we shall see in this rabble gathered at the mountain the foreshadowing of a remade world. From Sinai we move to Jerusalem, to see how the foreshadowed remaking of the world develops with the promises of God's king given to David. Jerusalem becomes a powerful symbol of a regathered world.

From Jerusalem, however, we must move to Babylon, a word which came to symbolise the scattering of God's people in exile. The historical Babylon became much more than a place; it became a reprise of all the scattering that the ancient Tower of Babel symbolised. By the time we have travelled from Eden through Babel, Sinai, and Jerusalem and then out to Babylon, we really do not seem to have made any progress. What kind of a story is it that spends so long getting us from Babel to Babylon? It becomes clear that Sinai and Jerusalem together are not the remaking of a broken world, but rather the foreshadowing and anticipation of the actual remaking, which is yet to come.

The story continues after Babylon until we come to the central event of human history, at Golgotha, the place of the Skull (the place where Jesus was crucified) (Matthew 27 v 33). This terrible unfair death, itself the epitome of what goes wrong in a broken world, turns out paradoxically to be the event around which a remade world will focus and the magnet which will draw all sorts of people together. From Golgotha we move to the first Christian Pentecost in Jerusalem, where the miraculous understanding of different human languages signifies the reversal of the babble of tongues that was Babel. Golgotha and Pentecost show us how the promises of gathering in the Old Testament will finally be made real in the church.

So from Pentecost we move to the local church, which is at the same time scattered all over the world and yet contains within itself the seeds of a worldwide gathering—local churches are scattered gatherings! We shall spend some time exploring how a local church is shaped around themes from Sinai and Jerusalem, while still suffering from being placed in a world east of Eden and in the long shadow of the Tower of Babel. We shall look at how the local church is made possible by the Cross and the gift of the Holy Spirit. Finally, from the scattered gathering that is the local church we follow the trajectory of grace to end our story with the New Jerusalem, a picture of the renewed Creation, a broken world remade at last to the glory of the God who is One. It is a great story.

## Questions for Discussion

1. Review what this chapter teaches about God. Why does the nature of God mean there ought to be harmony in the world?
2. Why does it matter so much that there should be harmony in the world?
3. What experiences do you have of the pain of a broken world? What behaviours have caused this brokenness?
4. What experiences do you have of relationships in a local church? Do people relate differently there, or not?

**ALL HUMANITY**

**EDEN:**
**Gathered in the Garden**

**BABEL:**
**Scattered by Pride**

# A Broken World:
# Scattered Without God

There can be no peace east of Eden. The purpose of this first main section (Chapters 1 and 2) is to persuade us of that. The garden of Eden is spoken of as having a gate "on the east side", and the expression "east of Eden" comes to be a figurative way of saying *outside the garden of Eden, alienated from fellowship with God, the land of wandering, where Cain wanders after murdering his brother Abel* (Genesis 3 v 24; 4 v 16).

Most people think that it is perfectly possible to enjoy harmony east of Eden, that human beings are well able to "do the peace and harmony thing" without bringing God into the picture. In fact quite a few people think that bringing God into the picture just makes things worse and causes strife. An opinion poll in Britain in 2006 showed that 82 per cent of adults "see religion as a cause of division and tension between people".[8] This is nothing new. The Roman poet Lucretius wrote that "Religion can incite so much evil".

In his song, "Imagine", John Lennon suggests that if there were no heaven (i.e. no religion) then we would have world peace because there would no longer be any cause to kill or to die for. Sir Elton John says that religion "turns people into hateful lemmings" (and would, incidentally, "ban religion completely"!).[9]

This is a common view, even though the careful historical analysis of Meic Pearse in his book *The Gods of War: Is Religion the Primary Cause of Violent Conflict?* shows that it is a simplistic and misleading cliché. The bloodiest wars in human history have been secular rather than religious, for a start. I want to persuade you that *apart from* fellowship with God no human community is stable.

It is interesting how much we like to dream of stability and harmony. A TV or radio series, such as *Friends, Suits, The West Wing* or *The Archers,* generally revolves around a small group of characters who spend a lot of time interacting with each other, and although there are tensions, by and large they stay together. From time to time a new character is introduced, or a character is removed from the series. But most of the time we love them because it's the same group and, by and large, even though they may spar with one another, they are loyal to one another. We love that dream.

That may also be why we continue to call a place "the village" long after it has been absorbed into a sprawling conurbation. I was brought up in Roehampton in south-west London, which has for a long time been part of a continuous urban sprawl. And yet Roehampton is still fondly called "the village", perhaps because we love the idea of a small and friendly place where everyone knows everyone and lives in happy harmony. Even though the reality may be proximity without intimacy, we dream of a world where there is intimacy and harmony.

But how is that dream to come true? How is a broken world to be remade? Can we manage it without God? Can we do it east of Eden? We can't: and until we are deeply persuaded that we can't, we will not wholeheartedly join in God's plan to remake it through the local church. So we must begin with the necessary demolition work of getting rid of our mistaken idea that we can do it on our own.

## ONE

# Eden: Expelled to Wander

We begin our Bible tour in "a garden in the east, in Eden" (Genesis 2 v 8). It is a short story—true, tragic and all too brief—the story of Adam and Eve in the garden of Eden with God. Two themes are tightly connected: harmony and husbandry (husbandry means something like gardening or farming). Adam and Eve are to live in harmony with God, with one another and with the created world that is placed in their care. They cannot look after the garden if they are fighting one another: husbandry needs harmony.

### In the Garden of Eden: the First Church (Genesis 2 v 4-25)

Our first Bible passage is Genesis 2 v 4-25. Before we look at it, we must glance at the passage before it, the very beginning of the Bible, Genesis 1 v 1 – 2 v 3. Here we are introduced to a wonderful world, repeatedly called "good", with God-given order and boundaries, and needing good human government. This is why the climax of this first drama is the creation of the man and the woman who are given the privilege and responsibility of looking after the world (1 v 26-28). Human beings are to be God-like creatures, made in his image and likeness, governing his world in harmony. Because they are God-like, and God is One, they and their family are to be one united humanity, governing together without strife.

This harmony is beautifully pictured in the story of the Garden of Eden, in Genesis 2. When Genesis speaks of a garden, we are to picture something like the large parkland surrounding a country house, rather than a little suburban patch of grass with a few flower beds. One of the first things that strikes us about this garden is its beauty. It is full of "all kinds of trees … that were pleasing to the eye and good for food" (v 9); this garden is both beautiful ("pleasing to the eye") and fruitful ("good for food"). Along with its beauty is its sheer abundance of life: "the tree of life" is in the middle of the garden, as a picture of the source of all created life (v 9). Life is also pictured by the language of water: the river that waters the garden then flows out into the world and is portrayed as the source of great rivers of the ancient Near East (v 10-14). When this garden is referred to elsewhere in the Old Testament it is spoken of as the very picture of beauty, life and loveliness. It is the opposite of ruins, deserts and waste-lands; it is a place of joy, gladness, thanksgiving and singing, a place that is "perfect in beauty".[10] In the north-west of England there is a very beautiful valley called "the Vale of Eden", echoing this same imagery.

There are two reasons why this garden is so full of life and beauty. The first is that this is the place where God walks on earth. We are not told this directly in Genesis 2, but in Genesis 3 v 8 we read of "the LORD God … walking in the garden in the cool of the day". The implication is that God took a delightful stroll in the garden evening by evening, when the fierce heat of the Middle Eastern day was past. Of course this uses human language, because this is the only language we can understand; we are not to think of God having feet! It's a way of telling us that God lives there. This is where he loves to walk. And because it is where God is, it is bound to be a place of unrivalled loveliness and delight.

But there is a second reason why Eden is a place of beauty and life. If we may say so with reverence, it is not enough that God walks there. The garden needs looking after: and God has decided not to look after it himself, or not directly. He has decided that human beings are going to look after it for him. Just before the story of the garden, we read of a time when "no shrub had yet appeared on the earth and no plant had yet sprung up". One of the reasons given for this lack of plants is that, "there was no one to work the ground" (2 v 5). So the grounds need a groundsman; the garden will not be really beautiful without a gardener. This is why "The LORD God took the man and put him in the Garden of Eden *to work it and take care of it*" (v 15). It is to be a well-cared-for garden, and Adam is to do it. There is an old story of a gardener resting on his spade after a hard spell of digging up weeds and planting shrubs in his garden. A minister comes by and says piously, "How lovely! God has made a very beautiful garden." To which the tired gardener replies, with a little edge in his voice, "Well, yes, it is beautiful, but you should have seen it when God had it to himself!"

It is a big job that Adam is given. It isn't good for him to be left to do it all on his own. This is why Eve is created, not just to be a lover and companion, but to be a "*helper* suitable for him", so that working together in harmony with God and one another they and their future family can care for God's parkland (v 18). In a way, we may say that Adam, Eve and God formed the first church, in the garden. It was a small church, but it contained within itself the seeds of a great worldwide assembly of men and women walking in fellow-ship with God and harmony with one another, caring for the world God made.

The picture so far in the Bible story is of a universe in which there is life, order, and harmony. In this universe the expression, "the heavens and the earth" simply means everything high and low, and all in between (Genesis 1 v 1). We might as well say, *East and West, and everything in between; the hot things and the cold things, the big things and the little things, the high things and the low things, and everything in between.* There are no barriers, no curtains, no walls, between heaven and earth. God walks with people on earth. This totality is all simply uniformly *good.* It is one harmonious whole, the theatre of the glory of God, singing back to him its praises, calling out with joy in his beauty, shining brightly his glory, the visible unclouded expression of his unseen being. What a beautiful world! What a great and good God! Heaven and earth together as one with no barriers of war or strife. This is the undivided "heavens and ... earth" pictured for us in the intimate assembly in the garden, between God, the man and the woman.

But here's a question: is God really still needed? Even if we assume he made it, is he still needed to hold it all together? Why can't Adam and Eve and their family run it perfectly well without him? They are God-like creatures, so surely they are up to the task, aren't they? To put it in con-temporary terms, why is God necessary for human harmo-ny? Why can't we live together perfectly well without God, and care for the world without bringing God into the equa-tion? When Tony Blair was British Prime Minister his Press Secretary Alistair Campbell famously said of the Government, "We don't do God"; many would say the moment we begin to "do God" in human affairs, we introduce strife. For example, according to Professor Hermann Bondi, writing in the magazine *Nature*, "The past as well as the present can leave no doubt that the variety of religions is a calamitously divisive force in human affairs. The less this factor is brought in, the better for all."[11] So wouldn't we do better just to leave God out of the picture and seek to build a free world on the basis of secular liberal humanism, for example?

At this stage in the story we have only a warning to go on to answer that. Before long, we shall have lots more evidence, but for the moment just this word. It's the warning we missed out. Just after God puts the man in the garden "to work it and take care of it", he commands him, "You are free to eat from any tree in the garden; but you must not eat from the tree of the knowledge of good and evil, for when you eat from it you will certainly die" (Genesis 2 v 16-17). What is this "tree of the knowledge of good and evil"? In Genesis 3 v 5 the snake tells them that if they eat it their eyes will be opened, and they "will be like God, knowing good and evil". In one sense, they are already "like God" as creatures made in God's image and likeness; but this fruit will make them rivals to God, knowing "good and evil" (which may be a way of saying "everything"). God says that if they set themselves up as rivals to God, they will die (Genesis 2 v 17). Instead of harmony there will be strife; instead of fruitfulness, deserts and wasteland; instead of life, death. But is God telling the truth? Can human beings really not live together and run the world perfectly well without bringing God into the picture? We shall see when the story continues outside the garden.

## East of Eden: Life Without God (Genesis 3-10)

Much of Genesis 3–10 is like the "Chamber of Horrors" in London's Madame Tussauds waxworks, the place where the most ugly and horrible exhibits are displayed. We shall walk through it quickly, pausing only to see examples of how human harmony is destroyed by the human decision to be rivals to God.

The first thing we see is alienation from God. After Eve and Adam have eaten the forbidden fruit, God comes into the garden for his regular evening walk, and seeks their company. But they hide in shame (3 v 8). From now on their relationship with God is broken.

The next thing we see is sinners portraying themselves as victims. Adam is asked to explain himself, and replies, "The woman you put here with me—she gave me some fruit from the tree, and I ate it" (3 v 12). When the woman is asked to explain herself, she blames the snake (3 v 13). *It is God's fault for putting the woman here; it is the woman's fault for giving me the fruit; it is the snake's fault.* But one thing we can be sure of: *it's not my fault!* There is a "Calvin and Hobbes" cartoon in which the boy Calvin says, "Nothing I do is my fault. My family is dysfunctional and my parents won't empower me! Consequently I'm not self-actualized! My behaviour is addictive functioning in a disease process of toxic co-dependency. I need holistic healing and wellness before I'll accept any responsibility for my actions!" The pet tiger Hobbes comments, "One of us needs to stick his head in a bucket of ice-water", and Calvin walks off saying, "I love the culture of victimhood."[12] So do we all: our first instinct is to blame someone else, just as Adam and Eve did.

We are not to imagine Adam and Eve leaving the garden arm in arm when God expelled them, to live happily ever after in cheerful independence of God. As someone said to me, it would be easy to think, "Well, at least they've got each other", even if it's a bit sad they're expelled from the garden. Had there been two gates out of Eden, we may be sure they would have stormed out of different ones, not speaking to each other, muttering under their breath how it was all the other's fault. A broken relationship with God leads to blaming other people.

The third signal we see that life without God is life without harmony is the story of Cain and Abel (Genesis 4 v 1-16). Adam and Eve have two sons. But before long, Cain murders his brother Abel. At the end of the story, Abel is dead, and Cain is condemned to be "a restless wanderer on the earth" (v 12), a scattered, frightened, vulnerable person, living in "the land of Nod" (which means "wandering") "east of Eden" (v 16). (So "east of Eden" becomes an expression meaning "outside the garden of Eden".) Instead of one united family governing God's world, we have a family broken by murder and riddled with guilt.

The American novelist John Steinbeck won the Nobel Prize for Literature for his haunting novel *East of Eden*, which sees the story of Cain and Abel as a terrible recurrent theme of human history.[13] Adam Trask, one of the main characters, has a Chinese cook called Lee, who turns out to be a thinker into whose mouth Steinbeck seems to put his own views. Adam Trask reads the sixteen-verse story of Cain and Abel to Lee, and for ten years Lee thinks about it. He recognizes that "these sixteen verses are a history of humankind in any age or culture or race". The question in Lee's mind is whether or how it is possible to escape this story. Lee's (and Steinbeck's) thinking focuses on the translation of something God says to Cain before the murder. In Genesis 4 v 7, God says, "if you do not do what is right, sin is crouching at your door; it desires to have you, *but you must rule over it*". Lee notices that the King James Version translates the Hebrew verb *timshel* by, "*thou shalt* rule over" sin, which he understands to be a promise that Cain will conquer sin. Another translation (like the NIV) reads it as a command: "you must rule over it". In fact our translations are right to read it as a command.[14] But Lee takes advice and comes up with the (linguistically incorrect) proposal that it ought to be translated "thou mayest", stressing the free choice that Cain has. He calls this "the most important word in the world", that human beings have to choose, and can freely choose, whether or not to sin, whether or not to live in harmony. The significance Steinbeck gives to this conversation becomes clear at the very end of the book, where the last word Adam Trask whispers on his deathbed is the Hebrew verb *timshel*. Steinbeck hints that the choice is ours: we are not locked into a cycle of "Cain and Abel" stories, but have the power to break free and choose differently. Underlying Steinbeck's suggestion is the thought that we can manage human harmony without God. Quite apart from the translation error, is he right? The evidence of human history suggests not.

Soon after Cain and Abel, the Chamber of Horrors continues with one of his descendants called Lamech (Genesis 4 v 18-24). Lamech is the first recorded bigamist; he has two wives, Adah and Zillah. The ugliest thing about Lamech is the way he boasts to them about revenge:

> Adah and Zillah, listen to me;
>> wives of Lamech, hear my words.
> I have killed a man for wounding me,
>> a young man for injuring me.
> If Cain is avenged seven times,
>> then Lamech seventy-seven times. (Genesis 4 v 23-24)

Someone has hurt him, and to prove that he is not a man to be messed with, he murders him and boasts about it. Lamech is Cain magnified, scattering multiplied, harmony shredded. Revenge works like this and always has. In the Roman baths in Bath, UK, archaeologists have uncovered some curses written in Latin. Here is one: "Docimedes has lost two gloves. He asks that the person who stole them should lose his mind and his eyes in the temple where she (the goddess) appoints." This is Lamech's attitude: You offend me, I break your leg. You hit me, I drop a bomb on you. You mock me, I hurt you with all my might. And the more might, the more out of all proportion my response, the more I can boast like Lamech that I am a man to be reckoned with. As the poet W.H. Auden expressed it,

I and the public know
What all school children learn,
Those to whom evil is done
Do evil in return.

This is what happens to human harmony east of Eden. By the time we reach Genesis 6, God looks at the earth and sees it "full of violence" (Genesis 6 v 11).

We have seen blame, murder, revenge and violence. But the worst and most deeply scattering result of alienation from God is death. *Don't eat the fruit*, God had said, "for when you eat from it you will certainly die" (2 v 17). And die they did, really, physically, bodily. The most common words in the genealogy of Noah in Genesis 5 are, "and then he died". Their bodies stopped breathing, the blood stopped circulating, their corpses were laid in the ground and began to rot. Paul sums this up in his letter to the church in Rome: "sin entered the world through one man, and death through sin, and in this way death came to all people, because all sinned" (Romans 5 v 12).

The denial of death is the devil's follow-up lie. His first lie was that we would not die: he follows this up today with the lie that denies the reality and seriousness of death. Some of the ways we swallow this lie are absurd. A portrait photographer was telling me of a family photo in which the family insisted on including an empty chair. When he asked why, the father replied, "That's for my Uncle Harry". "So where is Uncle Harry?" asked the photographer. "Oh, he's dead," came the reply. They produced an old photo of Uncle Harry and insisted on him being pasted in to the family group. But whatever the wonders of digital photography, Uncle Harry was not there because Uncle Harry was dead. That is the truth.

Sometimes we speak of "spiritual death" as the separation from God which happened immediately when Adam and Eve disobeyed. The Bible does sometimes speak in these terms. But the Bible's main emphasis is on the bodily physical death that inevitably follows from separation from God, sooner or later. God did not just promise some kind of spiritual alienation from him: he promised that their bodies would die. And when their bodies died, *they* died. You and I have no substantial existence apart from our bodies; we are embodied people.

The best-selling non-fiction book on Amazon in February 2008 was *A New Earth: Awakening to Your Life's Purpose* by Eckhart Tolle, a book whose sales have been helped (to put it mildly) by being recommended by Oprah Winfrey. In February and March 2008 Penguin were printing a million copies a week to meet demand.[15] The philosophy that drives this "New Age" book is an old one, familiar to historians and philosophers from Buddhism. Our bodies give us an illusory sense of self, we are told. But at a deeper level, the level of the "spirit" (which is currently "imprisoned in matter"), underneath the surface, actually "everything is ... connected with everything else". Actually everything is connected as one indivisible whole. All we have to do is to allow our consciousness to flower so that we become enlightened and sense our "connectedness with the whole". Our bodies, our Ego, all forms, are illusory: formlessness is reality.[16]

Every mourner at a funeral knows, when the body of someone they love is lowered into the ground or put into the crematorium fire, that this is make-believe. Philosophies and religions that replace the bodily world by an immaterial "spiritual" world are strategies to pretend that God's judgment on human sin has not happened.

I came across a website inviting bereaved people to send in "a poem you found particularly helpful" (never mind if it was true or not). One poem read like this:

Do not stand at my grave and weep;
I am not there. I do not sleep.
I am a thousand winds that blow;
I am diamond glints of snow;
I am the sunlight on ripened grain;
I am the gentle autumn's rain.
When you awaken in the morning's hush;
I am the swift uplifting rush
of quiet birds encircled flight.
I am the soft star that shines at night.
Do not stand at my grave and cry;
I am not there, I did not die.

Eckhart Tolle would have liked that one. My existence as an individual is an illusion: so all that happens when I die is that, like a chicken stock cube melting into a saucepan of soup, I am absorbed back into the cosmic soup.

Then there is the famous poem from Henry Scott-Holland, which begins, "Death is nothing at all. I have only slipped into the room next door. I am I, and you are you…" But it's not true. If you are around when I die and someone suggests saying that poem at my funeral, please point out to them that if I have really "slipped into the room next door" I have carelessly managed to leave my body behind! I will be separated from those who love me, and they from me. We will be scattered and no amount of philosophical make-believe will gather us in this life: so please feel free to weep for the scattering of a broken world.

Death scatters and separates human beings most cruelly of all. It separates spirit from body and the living from the dead. It separates with no hope of reconciliation; it breaks human fellowship and harmony for ever. The snake said it wouldn't happen, but it did happen and it has gone on happening ever since (Genesis 3 v 4). It is wishful thinking to say that all men and women who have died are "united in death" or "reunited at last". No, outside of Jesus, they are scattered and separated for ever by death. There is no camaraderie beyond the grave. Even if men and women were able to learn to live in harmony on earth without God, they would still be scattered by death. Death is what God promises in Genesis 2 to those who are alienated from him: and in death we are necessarily and finally separated from one another. There is no such thing as lasting human harmony apart from fellowship with God.

In this quick tour through Genesis 1 to 10 I have missed out the little hints of hope, the anticipations of the good news of Jesus. They are there: one day Eve's descendant will crush the serpent's head; even outside the garden people begin to worship God, as Abel does; Cain is not given the full punishment for his sin, so this world of wandering is not hell because evil is restrained; Enoch mysteriously does not die; Noah is a kind of saviour-figure and his Ark a place of safety.[17] So we are encouraged to read on! But all these signs of hope relate to what God promises and God does; none of them encourage us to think we human beings can live in lasting harmony by ourselves.

## Questions for Discussion

1. Review the Bible teaching in this chapter. How does Genesis 3 to 10 portray broken human relationships outside the garden of Eden?
2. In what ways have you seen relationships damaged when we refuse to accept blame?
3. What experience do you have of revenge making broken relationships worse?
4. How does our society show it thinks it can make peace among human beings without reference to God?
5. How does strife in the world threaten the glory of God?

## TWO

# Babel: Scattered
# by Pride

The next stopping point on our Bible tour is in some ways the climax of the Chamber of Horrors. It concludes the portrait in Genesis 3 to 11 of a broken world. It gives the iconic answer to the question we have been considering: Is human harmony possible east of Eden? Can human beings manage the "living together in peace" thing on their own?

A young woman told me once that one of the factors that finally led her to Christian faith was her teenage experience of trying to make peace between her quarrelling parents. Again and again, it seems, she found herself in the midst of strife in the home. She had assumed that if only she could get her parents to sit down together over the proverbial English cup of tea, then she could help them sort out their differences. It was the gradual realisation that she couldn't that led her to look outside of herself for rescue and reconciliation.

We are going to pause now at one of the most famous Bible stories, the Tower of Babel (Genesis 11 v 1-9). This story helps us understand just why peace outside Eden will always be fragile and temporary, and no stable human society, marriage or family is possible while human beings are alienated from the God who is One.

The Tower of Babel is not recounted in its chronological place in the story. Already in Genesis 10 we have been told of different people groups dispersed through the world, and with different languages (v 5, 20, 31, 32). It may be that it happened at the time when "the earth was divided" (10 v 25); we cannot be sure. Immediately after the Tower of Babel, in Genesis 11 v 10, we begin the genealogy that leads to Abraham and the story of Abraham's people, the great Bible story of promise and rescue. Babel seems to be placed at the end of the first section of Genesis because it sums up the human condition after expulsion from the presence of God. Scattering and ruptured community is endemic to that condition. There really is no peace east of Eden.

## The Tower of Babel (Genesis 11 v 1-9)

Now the whole world had one language and a common speech. As people moved eastward, they found a plain in Shinar and settled there.

They said to each other, "Come, let's make bricks and bake them thoroughly." They used brick instead of stone, and bitumen for mortar. Then they said, "Come, let us build ourselves a city, with a tower that reaches to the heavens, so that we may make a name for ourselves; otherwise we will be scattered over the face of the whole earth."

But the Lord came down to see the city and the tower the people were building. The Lord said, "If as one people speaking the same language they have begun to do this, then nothing they plan to do will be impossible for them. Come, let us go down and confuse their language so they will not understand each other."

So the Lord scattered them from there over all the earth, and they stopped building the city. That is why it was called Babel—because there the Lord confused the language of the whole world. From there the Lord scattered them over the face of the whole earth.

This carefully constructed passage begins with one language (v 1) and ends with confused languages (v 9); it begins with one group of people (v 2) and ends with a scattered rabble (v 9).

Verse 1 emphasises by repetition that they had "one language" and "a common (i.e. shared) speech". This looks like humanity in harmony. They spoke the same language. We use exactly this expression today in a metaphorical sense as well as a literal sense. So we might say of someone, "she and I speak the same language". We don't just mean that we both speak in Portuguese, for example: we mean we really understand one another. We can work together; this is someone we can "do business with".

In verse 2 we are to picture a representative group of this seemingly harmonious humanity moving eastward and finding a flood plain in Shinar (that is, Babylonia), and settling there. Later, in exile, the Jews knew this plain at first hand, exiled to Babylon on the flood plain of the river Euphrates. Indeed the whole story is told in such a way that it becomes a sharply ironic polemic against Babylonian life, politics and religion. It is not a story you would want the Babylonian police to find on your laptop! It would have been what in the Soviet Union was called *samizdat* (i.e. underground) literature.

It is only when these people begin to speak (in their shared language) that we see what is going on in their hearts:

"Come, let's make bricks and bake them thoroughly" (v 3). And the narrator comments, "They used brick instead of stone, and bitumen for mortar". On the flood plain there was no stone, so they baked bricks. This seems innocent enough, but the exiles in Babylon knew that this was precisely the building construction used by Nebuchadnezzar's builders. Some of his carefully baked bricks have been excavated. This old story echoed down the ages and would have reminded the Jews especially of Nebuchadnezzar's Babylon.

But why are they working together to bake bricks? Verse 4 gives their motivation: "Come, let us build ourselves a city, with a tower that reaches to the heavens, so that we may make a name for ourselves; otherwise we will be scattered over the face of the whole earth."

Again, they still did this centuries later in Nebuchadnezzar's Babylon, following an ancient tradition of ziggurats, which were temples built up flights of stairs as high as technology would carry them, with the house of the god as near to heaven as it could be.

The purpose of the Tower of Babel is to tie the city to the heavens and to enable the people to rule the world like gods. This is not human beings wanting *access* to gods above them: it is human beings wanting themselves *to be in the place of* the gods. They do not climb to worship the gods, but to "make a name for *ourselves*" (v 4). One scholar sums it up like this: "what we have here is an account in which all the God-given abilities of human beings are deliberately focused on creating a society where God is redundant … the inhabitants of this human city view the creator as irrelevant".[18] But notice how anxious they are ("otherwise we will be scattered"). It is not clear whether they are simply anxious not to do what God wants (to spread through the earth) or—as seems more likely—that they are anxious about human community becoming confused and broken. We might even picture them as an ancient "peace movement" encouraging cooperation, working together on a shared project, a kind of proto-United Nations. But they do it in order to make God redundant: they use man-made religion as an instrument of social control (to keep the empire united) and therefore precisely what they fear comes upon them.

In Babylon, the tower was religion being used as an instrument of social control, as it has so often been in the history of the world. This was the purpose of the great Khmer temples (most famously Angkor Wat), to keep the people subservient under the unifying power of religion of which the king was in charge. This was the purpose of the Roman imperial cult, where the emperor himself was to be worshipped as divine. This was the use of human religion mocked by Karl Marx in his famous expression, "the opiate of the masses".

They want to be a united humanity living in autonomy, making their own decisions, running their world the way they want, with no need for gods or goddesses above them. The Tower of Babel is a symbol of human autonomy and pride.

But the great point of the story is that there can be no harmony except under God. With wonderful irony the storyteller says, "But the LORD came down to see the city and the tower the people were building" (v 5). He had to come *down* to look at this magnificent "heavenly" construction; it doesn't even reach close enough to heaven for him to see it clearly. We are to picture him peering down, asking, *What is that little dot I can just see? Ah, well, I'd better go down and have a look.* How pathetic it is, this tower made by humans wanting to run the world independently of God.

When he sees the tower, God's reaction is parallel to his reaction when Adam and Eve had eaten from the forbidden tree. In Eden he said to himself, "The man has now become like one of us, knowing good and evil. He must not be allowed to reach out his hand and take also from the tree of life and eat, and live for ever" (Genesis 3 v 22). At Babel he says, "If as one people speaking the same language they have begun to do this, then nothing they plan to do will be impossible for them. Come, let us go down and confuse their languages so they will not understand each other" (Genesis 11 v 6-7).

Both of these reactions by God, in Eden and at Babel, look on the face of it as if God felt threatened and reacted defensively as an insecure human ruler might, lashing out at opponents to try to make his position more secure. The difference is that this ruler is the God who is One, the creator of the world. God cannot allow his "God-ness" to be challenged without the integrity of the universe being broken. What for us would be insecurity and arrogance, for God is utterly necessary and appropriate: he simply must ensure that his divine rule is unchallenged. The universe would fall apart if he did not. God cannot allow human beings to succeed in playing at God. The objective fact is that he is the only true God, the creator and sustainer of the universe.

When God says, "then nothing they plan to do will be impossible for them", I take it this is hypothetical: God is saying if he allows rebellion to go unchallenged and unconstrained, there will be no limit to the reach of evil. So he acts with divine sovereignty to frustrate them. He does this, not by sending thunderbolts to destroy the tower, but in a much more profound way: he confuses their languages, so their harmony is frustrated and they can no longer understand one another and work together.

The result is scattering: "So the LORD scattered them from there over all the earth, and they stopped building the city" (not only the tower) (v 8). "That is why it was called Babel" (which means "Babylon", but also sounds like the Hebrew word for "confused", rather like our word "babble") "because there the LORD confused the language of the whole world. From there the LORD scattered them over the face of the whole earth" (v 9), which was precisely what they were trying to avoid (in verse 4). The great Babylon, the symbol of human initiative, technological wonder, and imperial success, is actually just "babble", the place of confusion and scattering. We shall come back to this in Chapter 5.

So the harmony of voices singing together in tune is replaced by a horrible raucous noise, each trying to shout louder in its own language with its own agenda. The orchestra have deposed the conductor and each is playing just what he or she feels like playing. And while their playing may be "true for them", the result is a noisy, chaotic and divided world. In what is virtually a commentary on the Tower of Babel, Mary the mother of Jesus sang that the mighty God "has scattered those who are proud in their inmost thoughts" (Luke 1 v 51).

## The Babel of a Broken World

The point of the Tower of Babel is not just that it happened: it is that it happens, and happens, and happens again. It is the shape of human society east of Eden. When the builders of Babel were scattered, they did not give up building towers: it is just that now they all tried to build their own towers! It is an irony that in some ways Babel goes on happening literally, as society after society seeks to build the tallest tower on earth. I remember going to an exhibition at the Royal Academy in London, of architects' models of very tall towers, several of which were at one time the tallest tower on earth.

As I write, the tallest artificial structure of all time is the Burj Khalifa, a colossal 828 metres high, like a huge hypodermic needle piercing the sky in Dubai. For Londoners, it may be helpful to say that it is the height of three Canary Wharfs plus one St Paul's Cathedral; for New Yorkers, two Chrysler Buildings plus two Statues of Liberty.

However, the main point is not that Babel is repeated literally: it is that it is happening all the time theologically. This is a profoundly theological story. Human harmony is only possible in loving relationship with God; it is never possible for human beings cut off from God, who are trying to be little gods and goddesses themselves. The moment I cut myself off from God and seek to "make a name" for myself, it is as if I set up business on my own. I have to fend for myself, look after "number one", watch my back, and mind my own business. No wonder the Bible says that "each of us has turned to our own way" (Isaiah 53 v 6).

All human relationships are affected. So I inevitably limit the kinds of contact I can have with you. I may have contact with you, but I will keep you at arm's length: otherwise if I get too close to you, your agenda will get mixed up with my agenda, and threaten my autonomy. And then I might have to make all sorts of compromises and even put your interests before my own, and I wouldn't want that. So I build my pathetic little Tower of Babel, and you build yours. The world is full of little "tower-builders", each of us constructing our own empire with me at the centre, me in the penthouse suite, and others existing only in relation to me and to serve me.

The more isolated I become, the more I become turned in on my own little world; Luther called this a world "curved in on itself". In a sense I develop my own language, rather as a people group isolated on an unreachable island will develop their own language independent of others on the mainland. And you develop your own language on your self-centred island. Before long, we have difficulty speaking and listening to one another. Like the stereotypical monoglot Englishman, I expect you to speak my language. And if you don't, I simply speak my own but a bit louder! I will not reach across the void in love to seek to understand yours. And in the same way you expect me to speak your language and will not reach out to speak mine. It is not long before the very possibility of a shared language, of objective reality, is denied. What is sometimes called "post-modernism" is as old as the Tower of Babel.

The result is fracture. We cannot live and work together. Every marriage struggles in the long shadow of the Tower of Babel; every relationship between parents and teenagers feels the darkness of incomprehension from Babel; every nation and people group struggles to get along with neighbouring people groups. In Europe we have a word for this—Balkanisation—which speaks of the disintegration especially characteristic of the Balkans. In modern times we have seen Yugoslavia tragically descend into civil war and chaos, with wars between and within its constituent parts—Serbia, Croatia, Bosnia, Kosovo, and so on. Balkanisation is the modern consequence of the Tower of Babel.

We live in a broken world. Here are two nearby headlines on foreign affairs in a journal: the first was about the fragility of Kenya and was entitled, "Next machetes, then machine guns?"; the second was about divisions within the Arab world and was called, "Can the Arab world's leaders stop bickering and help forge peace in the region?"[19] Headlines like this could be replicated week after week. A British diplomat has entitled a book *The Breaking of Nations*.[20] His thesis is that the biggest danger facing the world is not a superpower getting out of control, but simply the outbreak of chaos and "failed states" like Somalia, but all around the world. As he points out, "It was not the well-organised Persian empire that brought about the fall of Rome, but the barbarians".[21] In more recent times, we might add that it was not the might of the USA that brought down the Soviet Union, but the force of its own internal contradictions. Far from seeing a new and harmonious world order, we continue to strive against the breakdown of order on every scale, from the international scene to dysfunctional families.

Indeed those two ends of the scale would appear to be connected. When the core structure of the family breaks down and sexual incontinence overflows outside of marriage, it is only a matter of time before whole societies break down. The historian J.D. Unwin studied 86 different societies spanning 5000 years. He found an unexpected and direct correlation between sexual continence and the ability of a society to grow and remain healthy. He concluded, "In human records there is no instance of a society retaining its energy after a complete new generation has inherited a tradition which does not insist on pre-nuptial and post-nuptial continence"; by this "insistence" we do not mean no one ever had sex outside marriage, for that would not be true of any civilization: we mean a society where there is no public consensus that approves of sex outside marriage. The historian Arnold Toynbee said that, "Of the twenty-two civilizations that have appeared in history, nineteen of them collapsed when they reached the moral state the United States is in now".[22]

It is no accident that Babel has become an icon of human fracturing and chaos. One famous reworking of the Babel theme is *The Library of Babel,* a short story by Jorge Luis

Borges.[23] Borges invents a gigantic library which contains every possible combination of twenty-five characters (letters) printed over forty lines (each of eighty characters) and 410 pages. Every combination of syllables in every human language is to be found somewhere. The librarians spend their lives searching for occasional snatches of meaning. After a lifetime wandering through identical rooms, the narrator comes to regard all the combinations as equally meaningful. Meaning dissolves, and the confusion of languages is complete.[24]

The fundamental reason that human community is so hard to create and so stressful to sustain is that, as the French atheist philosopher Jean-Paul Sartre put it, "Man is the being whose project is to be God". By nature you and I want and plan and aspire to be God. *Well*, you say, *that's a bit of an overstatement. I mean, I'm just little old me. It's a bit rough, a bit grand, to accuse me of having as my life project the aspiration to be God.* But it's true, because by nature I stand at the centre of my world. You exist in relation to me. I assess you, I value you, according as you meet my needs, do my will, promote my comfort, and boost my ego. And so by nature I build a little empire of autonomy, of me making my choices, centred on me. It is true that I may not get very far in my project to be God. I may not succeed in building a very big empire. But I want to; that's my project, by nature. This is why we cannot live stably together.

## How is a Broken World to be Remade?

So, if we live in a broken world in which strife is endemic and meaning is unstable, how is this world to be remade, without having to resort to bringing God onto the stage? Can we human beings do it on our own?

## Apartheid

One notorious theological answer is to say that it doesn't need to be remade: instead we may use the Bible's narrative of a broken world as a mandate for the superiority of one race over another. Tragically this was done by parts of the Dutch Reformed Church in South Africa in the apartheid years, using the curse on Ham to justify the political policy euphemistically called "separate development" (Genesis 9 v 18-27). But, as Desmond Tutu eloquently and courageously declared to a Government commission of inquiry into the churches in 1981, the breakdown of human community at Babel "is the ultimate consequence according to the Bible of sin, separation, alienation, apartness," and, "It is a perverse exegesis that would hold that the story of the Tower of Babel is a justification for racial separation, a divine sanction for the diversity of nations. It is to declare that the divine punishment for sin had become the divine intention for mankind."[25]

## Multiculturalism

In recent years in the UK the strategy known as "multiculturalism" is—paradoxically—a first cousin of "separate development", but without the structural inequalities of apartheid. To make different ethic minorities feel at home in society, we were encouraged to affirm them in their diversity and plan for them to continue in their diversity with no expectation of any cultural convergence. And yet one of its former advocates, Jonathan Sacks, the former UK Chief Rabbi, wrote: "Multiculturalism has run its course, and it is time to move on. It was a fine, even noble idea in its time. It was designed to make ethnic and religious minorities feel more at home in society ... It affirmed their culture. It gave dignity to difference" and yet it hasn't worked: "It has led not to integration but to segregation ... It was intended to promote tolerance. Instead, the result has been ... societies more abrasive, fractured and intolerant than they once were."[26]

### Brute force

We must reject apartheid and we must admit that multiculturalism has failed. A third option, probably the most popular in the history of the world, is brute force.

In the eighth century BC, Assyria was the mighty power of the Ancient Near East. Their kings dreamed dreams of world dominion. The prophet Isaiah summed up these dreams of the king of Assyria like this:

> By the strength of my hand I have done this,
>     and by my wisdom, because I have understanding.
> I removed the boundaries of nations,
>     I plundered their treasures;
>     like a mighty one I subdued their kings.
> As one reaches into a nest,
>     so my hand reached for the wealth of the nations;
> as people gather abandoned eggs,
>     so I gathered all the countries;
> not one flapped a wing,
>     or opened its mouth to chirp. (Isaiah 10 v 13-14)

It is all "I" and "my". The king of Assyria boasted of his great power. He could move the boundaries of nations, uproot them, absorb them, plunder their treasures. It was as easy as collecting abandoned birds' eggs: no one could resist him. But the Assyrian empire came to an end.

The next regional superpower was the neo-Babylonian empire. Nebuchadnezzar was king of Babylon in its glory days (605-562 BC). He too dreamed dreams of world domination.

As he walked on the roof of his palace in Babylon, he said, "Is not this the great Babylon I have built as the royal residence, by my mighty power and for the glory of my majesty?" Again, it is all "I" and "my"; and yet the great proud Nebuchadnezzar was humbled (Daniel 4 v 29-33). Not very long after his death his empire was absorbed into the empire of the Medes and Persians. Before many centuries had passed Babylon itself had disappeared from view, until it began to be excavated from deep beneath the desert dust in the early 1900s.

Alexander the Great is said to have wept because there were no more worlds to conquer. And yet almost immediately on his death in 330 BC his empire fragmented, never to hold together again.

In 2008 the British Museum brought some of the famous Terracotta Army figures from China to London. The exhibition told some of the fascinating history of the Emperor Qin Shi Huang who unified China in 221 BC. It was an amazing story of military technology and organisational brilliance—and brute force. He unified China with an army of 700,000 slave soldiers and labourers, many of whom died in the project. Qin claimed, in a remarkable inscription in 219 BC, "The August Divine Emperor has unified cosmic power over the universe". He recognised that putting the world together is what gods try to do. Because he had done it, he claimed to be god. But he did it by force, and so the moment he died the whole thing fell apart.

A considerable part of the Pacific basin was "unified" under Japanese rule between 1942 and 1945. The background to this followed the restoration of the Meiji dynasty in Japan in 1861; there arose a strong militaristic movement, which led directly to the horrors of the Second World War in the Far East. Close by the Imperial Palace in Tokyo lies the Yasukuni Shrine, a

Shinto shrine where the two million Japanese war dead are remembered and worshipped (including 14 Class A war criminals hanged for their crimes), and where right-wing Japanese pray for their souls. Next to the shrine is a museum which tells history from a militaristic viewpoint. Its declared purpose is "to honour the courageous soldiers who laid the foundation for modern Japan, and to pray for the repose of their souls". The quotations on the walls include this one:

We shall die in the sea,
We shall die in the mountains
In whatever way,
We shall lie beside the Emperor,
never turning back.[27]

I suppose we could say that between 1942 and 1945 a part of the world was "united" under Japanese rule. But what a terrible kind of unity that was, and how immediately it was shattered at the end of the war.

### Voluntary cooperation

Force will never remake a broken world, because force uses the same instrument that is used to break the world in the first place. Evil can never be overcome by a greater evil. So, if force cannot achieve it, how about voluntary cooperation?

After the First World War (the so-called "Great War") of 1914-1918/9, the League of Nations was formed to foster voluntary cooperation between nations and ensure that this would indeed be what the British Prime Minister David Lloyd George hoped it would be "the war to end all wars".[28] But, as we know, two decades later the world was plunged into the Second World War which ended only with the explosion of two atom bombs, among the most terrible and powerful weapons ever invented in the history of the human race. Then, after that war ended, the United Nations was formed, and this continues to seek to prevent war; and yet wars go on and deaths mount, seemingly without end. In a revealing and courageous address to the World Council of Churches in 1954, Dag Hammarskjold (the second Secretary General of the United Nations, 1953-1961) said the Cross of Jesus is the one place where nations can be truly united nations.[29]

## Globalisation

In recent years it has sometimes been suggested that "globalisation" will reunite a broken world. This word is usually understood to have an economic dimension, focused on nations choosing to reduce tariff barriers, and a political dimension, the spread of a secular liberalism with its roots in philosophers such as John Stuart Mill. As travel becomes easier and telecommunications more widespread, so the world shrinks into a "global village" and culture becomes homogenised. In some versions of this vision, democracy spreads its blessings everywhere.

Free trade sounds very nice, and most nations can agree in theory that it is the best way for economies to cooperate and interact. But when resources are scarce, it is frightening how quickly economic theory surrenders to national self-interest. Nationalistic protectionism rears its ugly head, because each nation wants to look after its own. International agreements are so painfully hard to reach: almost everyone agrees that we should cooperate to reduce carbon emissions, but how hard it is to secure agreement actually to do this. This too is a legacy of the Tower of Babel.

When it comes to liberal democracy, one difficulty is that not every community wants it, and those to which it is "given" (or upon whom it is imposed) may throw up governments not at all to the liking of those who gave them this form of government. The historian Francis Fukuyama admitted in 1992 that "the broad acceptance of liberalism, political or economic, by a large number of nations will not be sufficient to eliminate differences between them based on culture".[30] The Brexit referendum, and the UK's subsequent protracted and difficult negotiations to leave the European Union, have shown that unity—both nationally and internationally—is hard to achieve. Globalisation is an attractive idea to some, but it means different things to different people and fails to be a recipe for uniting a broken world.[31]

## Conclusion: No Peace East of Eden

All human community is fragile and must always be fragile so long as it is the project of human beings without God. The great lesson from Eden to Babel is that until and unless God remakes his broken world, that world cannot be healed; it cannot heal itself. This is why the Bible story is so important for all of us who feel the pain of a broken world and long for harmony and peace.

The sad but sober truth is that the Tower of Babel speaks again and again of the ultimate futility of all purely human attempts to rebuild a broken world, to learn to speak "one language", to build together cooperatively in a way that makes a name for human beings as the architects of their own salvation. All human community on every scale struggles in the long shadow of the Tower of Babel.

Of course it is true that not all human community fragments and falls apart all the time. This world is not hell on earth. Human beings do make marriages that last; there are families that hold together; some nations stay together for a while, and even empires last for some years. God in his kindness restrains evil: the forces that fracture are not given unlimited sway. If they were, this world would be hell itself. Is human harmony possible east of Eden? Yes, but it is always fragile, never stable, always followed sooner or later by scattering.

So the question is: can the fragmentation of the world be not just restrained, but actively reversed? It is one thing for a terrible virus to be slowed down (as HIV/AIDS is with anti-retroviral drugs) but is there an active antidote to Babel, something that will not just slow down fracture but actually act as a cure? Is there a place where we see the scattering of Babel, not just slowed or restrained, but actually replaced by gathering?

The wonder of the Christian good news is that there is. Reconciliation with God is not just a nice mystical personal experience or a pietistic "plus" to add something extra to life: it is the precondition for stable human community. Where reconciliation with God is found, there human community begins actively to be rebuilt. The authentic local church contains the DNA of a remade world. But that is to run ahead of ourselves: before we get to that, God needs to educate us as he educated Old Testament Israel, about how he is going to rebuild a broken world. It is to that education that we now turn.

## Questions for Discussion

1. Review the Bible teaching in this chapter. Why is it important that God scatters the proud?

2. Look again at the strategies people have tried in order to make peace without God. Can you think of any others, or of examples of these?

3. When have you found it hard really to understand someone, or they found it hard to understand you? Why do you think this is?

4. What experience do you have of relationships being difficult because of cultural obstacles?

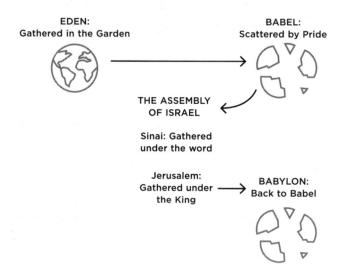

ALL HUMANITY

EDEN:
Gathered in the Garden

BABEL:
Scattered by Pride

THE ASSEMBLY
OF ISRAEL

Sinai: Gathered
under the word

Jerusalem:
Gathered under
the King

BABYLON:
Back to Babel

# The Assembly of Israel: Gathering Foreshadowed

So far we have been considering the universal human condition. The story of Eden and Babel concerns all human beings everywhere, scattered by pride, living without God and without peace in God's world. It has been both universal and depressing. We human beings cannot build stable community and harmony on our own. Our scattering is restrained by the kindness of God, so that this world is not hell; but there is, at this stage of the story, no active process clearly at work to put scattering into reverse and replace it by gathering. The world is like a patient receiving drugs to slow the onset of a degenerative illness, but without, at this stage, any treatment to put the illness into reverse and effect a cure.

When we begin the main rescue plot of the Bible at the end of Genesis 11 we find ourselves reading a much more local story. The story of Israel is about one man, one promise, one people in one place, not all peoples in the whole world. Paradoxically, it is the story we need to read if we are to understand how God is going to remake the whole world.

In this next section of our Bible tour we focus on the Assembly of Israel, the way God gathers his people together.

Our first main stop will be at Mount Sinai, where the Ten Commandments were given, and then we shall move to Jerusalem for the regular assemblies of the people of God through Israel's history. But tragically this section of the story ends back where we ended the first section, in Babylon (that is, Babel). The main part of the Bible story of Israel ends with scattering, just as the universal human condition is one of scattering.

We shall see the Assembly of Israel is not the way God actually and finally brings the world together. In some ways it is like a training exercise. Sometimes people being trained for something very important, such as special service troops or firefighters, will be taken through a realistic training exercise, so that when they meet the real thing they will recognize it and know how to respond. The Assembly of Israel is not the actual way God will rebuild his broken world but it teaches us lessons about how he will actually do it, so that we identify the real assembly when it happens.

# THREE

# Sinai: Gathered Under the Word

God gathers the world by speaking. That is only part of the truth, but it is an important part, and it is the focus of the first clearly defined God-called gathering east of Eden, which is the subject of this chapter. When God called the people of Israel together at Mount Sinai, he patterned there some of the critical features of the assemblies of the people of God in every age. But before we get to Sinai we need to trace some salient points in the journey from Babel to Sinai.

## From Babel to Sinai

### A. God promises to remake a broken world

Immediately after the Tower of Babel passage, the rest of Genesis 11 (v 10-32) gives a family line from Noah's son Shem (from whom we get the word "Semitic"). The particular line of interest is the one that leads to Abram (later called Abraham). The story that now begins is going to be God's remedy for the disaster of Babel. But it's a long story, and we won't see Babel reversed until the first Christian Pentecost many centuries later when people who spoke different languages all understood one another (Acts 2 v 1-13).

The story begins with God announcing the gospel to Abraham. After calling him to go "to the land I will show you", God says to him:

I will make you into a great nation,
    and I will bless you;
I will make your name great,
    and you will be a blessing.
I will bless those who bless you,
    and whoever curses you I will curse;
and all peoples on earth
    will be blessed through you. (Genesis 12 v 1-3)

In his letter to the churches in Galatia (part of modern Turkey), the apostle Paul says that when God said the climax of this ("all peoples on earth will be blessed through you"), he "announced the gospel in advance to Abraham" (Galatians 3 v 8). Paul goes on to explain that this will be fulfilled through Abraham's "seed" (singular) not his "seeds" (plural). But he then makes it clear that this singular "seed" doesn't just mean one solitary man (Jesus Christ), but one man who becomes the head of a new humanity: if we belong to this one seed (Jesus Christ) then all of us corporately "are Abraham's seed, and heirs according to the promise" (see Galatians 3 v 16 with v 29). So the gospel is God's promise to Abraham that through his descendant the whole world will be blessed. It is very important to get an accurate understanding of what this promise means, because it echoes down the centuries and is, in many ways, the driving force of the whole Bible story.

In the following chapters of Genesis the promise is repeated again and again. God tells Abraham that his family will be as many as the stars in the bright Middle-Eastern sky or the grains of sand on the beach, a family so big that no one can count them

(Genesis 15 v 5; 22 v 17). This is the family John, the writer of Revelation, sees in his vision centuries later, "a great multitude that no one could count, from every nation, tribe, people and language" (Revelation 7 v 9). God promises Abraham that he will be "the father of many nations" and that "kings will come" from him (Genesis 17 v 4-8). Through Abraham's descendant "all nations on earth will be blessed" (22 v 18).

God goes on and on repeating this promise all the way through Genesis, first to Abraham's promised son Isaac, and then to Isaac's chosen son Jacob, renamed Israel (whose children are called "the children of Israel" or "the Israelites"). Three times God uses an important word, the Hebrew word *qahal*, which means an assembly or a gathering. When Isaac blesses Jacob he says, "May God Almighty bless you and make you fruitful and increase your numbers until you become a *community* [literally "an assembly, a gathering, a *qahal*"] of peoples. May he give you and your descendants the blessing given to Abraham" (Genesis 28 v 3-4). Later God says to Jacob, "I am God Almighty; be fruitful and increase in number. A nation and a *community* [assembly] of nations will come from you, and kings will be among your descendants" (35 v 11). Jacob uses this same language when he tells Joseph's sons the promise, and includes these words: "I am going to make you fruitful and increase your numbers. I will make you a *community* [assembly] of peoples" (48 v 4). The psalms look forward to the great day when:

> The nobles of the nations *assemble*
>> as the people of the God of Abraham,
> for the kings of the earth belong to God;
>> he is greatly exalted. (Psalm 47 v 9)

One day there will be the promised worldwide assembly to the God of Abraham. So Abraham's family is not going to become a large number of isolated individuals: it is going to become a gathering, a great assembly from all the peoples of the world. It is going to be a broken world remade. This is the gospel.

This gospel promise is much much bigger than just a plot of land in what we now call the Middle East. When Paul sums it up in a nutshell he says the promise was "that he would be heir of the world" (Romans 4 v 13). It is the promise of a reassembled world. The peoples scattered at Babel will finally be regathered in Abraham's descendant. This promise drives the Bible storyline.

*B. Abraham's growing family is the nucleus of a reassembled world*
Genesis 12–50 tells the story of Abraham's family. It is a far from ideal family. Those of us who struggle with difficulties in our own families can take encouragement by reading the story of the wildly dysfunctional family God used to begin his remaking of a broken world! In his excellent book about Joseph, Liam Goligher draws attention to the wonderful reconciliation in Jacob's family by the end of Genesis. He writes:

> At the beginning [of Genesis] there is a family torn by murder [Cain and Abel]; at the end a family reunited by grace. At the beginning are people excluded from the Garden of Eden; at the end a people given a land that is a faint echo of Eden. At the beginning humanity is confronted with real guilt; at the end humanity learns of God's purpose to forgive. It is the New Testament which explains how such a transformation is possible. It points to Christ, who is the great reconciler. It points to the creation of a new society where sinners are welcomed in and restored by the healing power of mercy and grace.[32]

By the time we reach the start of the book of Exodus there are seventy descendants of Jacob (Exodus 1 v 1-5). It may not seem many, but this is the family to watch if we want to see the world put together again. And yet, for all the wonderful reconciliation at the end of Jacob's life, it is still a dysfunctional family again as the story continues. It is not yet the end of the story.

### C. God begins to keep his promise as Abraham's family grows to a redeemed rabble

The seventy descendants of Jacob multiply greatly, so that the land of Egypt is filled with them (Exodus 1 v 6-7). So the promise is beginning to be fulfilled, in the rather limited sense that Abraham is now the father of a substantial number of people. The problem is that they are hardly an assembly of people; rather they are a scattered group of slaves in Egypt who happen to have a shared ancestry. There are now lots of them, but in their character and relationships they are no different from the original humanity scattered from Babel.

Exodus 1–15 records how God redeemed this rabble from slavery in Egypt and brought them out in what we call the Exodus. They were a motley crew: Israelite men, women and children, with all sorts of hangers-on, to say nothing of the animals (12 v 37-38). They are certainly not a harmonious community: they grumble, they argue, and they have so many disputes that Moses is worn out by them (see Exodus 13–18 and especially 18 v 13-18). A generation later, when they are on the edge of the land, Moses remembers what it was like:

> At that time I said to you, "You are too heavy a burden
> for me to carry alone. The LORD your God has increased
> your numbers so that today you are as numerous as the

stars in the sky. May the LORD, the God of your ancestors, increase you a thousand times and bless you as he has promised! But how can I bear your problems and your burdens and your disputes all by myself?

(Deuteronomy 1 v 9-12)

They are a very long way from being the ordered harmonious assembly that will be the nucleus of a reassembled world. They are beginning to be gathered, but they still have within themselves the seeds of scattering: it is a miracle they stay together at all.

And so we come to the first God-given assembly of the people of God, where God gathers his people by speaking.

## The Church at Mount Sinai: God's People are Gathered under God's Voice

When God brought Israel out of Egypt he gave them, as it were, a one-way ticket to the Promised Land. But it was not to be a direct journey: they had to travel via Sinai. Years before, Moses was commissioned at Sinai for his job of leading the Exodus. God tells him, "When you have brought the people out of Egypt, you will worship God on this mountain", that is Mount Sinai (Exodus 3 v 12—Horeb in verse 1 is another word for Sinai). They had to go first to Sinai for a day that changed the world. They had to learn to assemble under the voice of God. God had this vital lesson to teach them: it is a lesson that must shape local church life today.

We read what happened when they reached Sinai, in Exodus 19 and 20, and Moses draws important lessons from it in Deuteronomy 4. The people camped around the edge of the mountain. When all was ready, the people came out of their tents and stood around the mountain and listened. The LORD came down to the top of the mountain; years before he had come down to the Tower of Babel to scatter proud people, but now he comes down with the purpose of gathering rather than scattering (Genesis 11 v 5; Exodus 19 v 20). Moses went up the mountain. Then God spoke, and the people heard his unmediated voice. It was an extraordinary and never-to-be-forgotten day. It teaches us at least six lessons, the first five of which ought to shape the local church.

## A. God redeems in order to assemble

God said to Moses, "Assemble the people before me" (Deuteronomy 4 v 10). The assembly was God's idea. God gathers. The people did not gather together and then decide it would be a good idea to invite God to join them (which is an impertinent idea). They gather because the God who loves to gather, gathers them. This is why he told Moses to bring them to the mountain. God gathers them, because God is in the business of remaking a broken world. This is what God loves to do. We see this same longing in the heart of God when he says in the psalms, "Gather to me my faithful ones"—that is, those set apart to belong to him (Psalm 50 v 5 ESV). He does not just want each of them individually close to him; he wants them to *gather* around him, in fellowship not just with him but with one another.

The word "church" simply means an assembly, a gathering, a congregation. What we see at Sinai is the first church east of Eden. Shortly before he died, Stephen, the first Christian martyr, referred to Israel as "the assembly [or "church"] in the desert" (Acts 7 v 38).[33] Later in Deuteronomy Moses three times refers to that day simply as "the day of the assembly":

1. "The LORD gave me two stone tablets inscribed by the finger of God. On them were all the commandments the

L ORD proclaimed to you on the mountain out of the fire, *on the day of the assembly*" (Deuteronomy 9 v 10).

2. After the episode of the golden calf Moses says that "The L ORD wrote on these tablets what he had written before, the Ten Commandments he had proclaimed to you on the mountain, out of the fire, *on the day of the assembly*" (10 v 4).

3. Reminding them that he had become God's spokesman (or prophet) to them, Moses says that "this is what you asked of the L ORD your God at Horeb *on the day of the assembly*" (18 v 16).

The Assembly of Israel on that great day became, in some respects, the standard shape of the assembly of the people of God in every age. We see covenant assemblies repeated at a number of points in the Old Testament.[34] Israel was defined as the assembly of the L ORD. Later assemblies are patterned on the day of that great prototype assembly.

The Assembly of Israel did not consist of whoever turned up for a meeting. It had a carefully defined membership; either someone was a member of the Assembly of Israel, or they were not (e.g. Deuteronomy 23 v 2-4). Indeed, an Israelite belonged to the Assembly even when they were not actually assembled. Israel is not a collection of individuals who sometimes assemble: it is an assembly whose members may sometimes be dispersed.

It is a wonderful thing to see Israel assemble here: for the first time in the Bible since the garden of Eden, there is a church in which God gathers his people and meets with them together. No wonder it was a day they never forgot! We need to remember when we gather in the local church that our assemblies are not just functional (to encourage us in our Christian lives); they are the reason God has redeemed us. He longs to have his people gathered to him and therefore to one another, because only then will they be the sign and foretaste of a remade world.

## B. God assembles all his people

Notice next that the Assembly at Sinai was the gathering of *all* God's people. Again and again in Deuteronomy, Moses addresses "all Israel" and expects future gatherings to be of "all Israel" (e.g. Deuteronomy 1 v 1; 31 v 1, 11). This theme continues in Israel's history and is especially emphasised by the writer of 1 and 2 Chronicles (e.g. 1 Chronicles 13 v 5). As the numbers grew, and when they were spread out in the Promised Land, it was not physically possible for every Israelite to assemble, and there must have been times when "all Israel" was a meeting of the senior representatives of Israel.

But the expression "all Israel" conveys a very important theological truth, which is that there is one people of God belonging to the one God. The God who is One must have one people: he cannot, by definition, have lots of separated and divided peoples. There is a distinction between Israel and the Gentiles, but there is to be no distinction within Israel; there are not to be two or more "Israels" (although, as we shall see, that is precisely what happened in Israel's history).

In our terms, there is to be a distinction between the church and the world; but there are not to be many separated churches. Of course, all over the physical world now there are different assemblies: but theologically there is one people of God, not many. The local church is to be the local expression of the whole people of God. This means that no local church should be deliberately particular or exclusive in the way it restricts itself to any one subset of the people of God, by gender (a church for men or a church for women), by race (a black church, a white church, an Asian church), by age (a church for the young, a church for the old), or by culture (a church for professionals, a church for the working class).

Having said this, we must remember that every church is built in the long shadow of the Tower of Babel. Language barriers are the most obvious manifestation of this: every church has to decide which language a meeting will be conducted in. And beyond this, all manner of cultural barriers are expressions of broader forms of language barriers. We joke that the British and the Americans are separated by a common language, and the same is true of all sorts of people within Britain or within America. We may speak the same language at one level, but all sorts of markers, idioms and accents within that language still serve to divide, as they do with every country. A church cannot avoid having some culture expressed in the way it meets and behaves; because of the fragmentation of human society, every church will inevitably reflect something of the specifics of where it is located: but every authentic church will begin to dilute, break down and undermine as many barriers as they can, as all the people of God are gathered by God's call.

### C. God assembles that we may hear and obey his voice

God gathers by speaking. God said to Moses, "Assemble the people before me *to hear my words*" (Deuteronomy 4 v 10). Not only is the assembly called together by the command of God, it is also gathered in order that they should hear and heed the word of God. The reason they gathered was not to look, but to listen. Moses stresses this:

> Remember the day you stood before the LORD your God at Horeb, when he said to me, "Assemble the people before me to hear my words so that they may learn to

revere me as long as they live in the land and may teach them to their children." You came near and stood at the foot of the mountain while it blazed with fire to the very heavens, with black clouds and deep darkness. *Then the LORD spoke to you out of the fire. You heard the sound of words but saw no form; there was only a voice.* He declared to you his covenant, the Ten Commandments, which he commanded you to follow and then wrote them on two stone tablets. And the LORD directed me at that time to teach you the decrees and laws you are to follow in the land that you are crossing the Jordan to possess. *You saw no form of any kind the day the LORD spoke to you* at Horeb out of the fire. (Deuteronomy 4 v 10-15)

Of course there were some things they saw: they saw the mountain burning with fire, they saw a deep darkness and cloud. But if you asked them later what they had seen, they would have said, *I don't really know what I saw—it had no shape or form—but I know exactly what I heard. I heard his voice. I heard the Covenant, the Ten Commandments.* Sinai was not so much a wonderful sight as an awesome and clear sound.

This teaches us that the reason we gather in church is first that we may hear and submit to the voice of God in his word. He assembles us by his command, and we assemble to listen to his word. The word of God is the driving force that shapes authentic church life. This is why the primacy of preaching and Bible teaching is not just one tradition amongst other equally valid Christian traditions: it is the defining mark of the assembly of the people of God. Unless our first desire when we gather is to hear and heed the voice of God in his word, we have missed the foundation point of church.

### D. Our relationships are to be shaped by the law of God so we can live together in peace

Only the word of God brings us together, and only the word of God can keep us together in harmony. The word of God is not an arbitrary exercise of God's authority, like God throwing his weight around to make sure we treat him with respect! The law of God is the only way of living that can enable human beings to live in peace. Unless our assemblies are shaped by the law of God they will never stay assembled.

What precisely they heard at Sinai was the Ten Commandments. The LORD "declared to you his covenant, the Ten Commandments, which he commanded you to follow and then wrote them on two stone tablets" (Deuteronomy 4 v 13). The Ten Commandments stand on their own level as the direct law of God, spoken unmediated by the voice of God at Sinai and written, as it were, directly by the finger of God on tablets of stone (a vivid way of speaking about them as directly from God himself) (9 v 10). They are put in the Ark (box) of the Covenant and sum up the covenant relationship between God and his people (10 v 5). Moses then expanded and applied these great commandments in detail to the corporate life of Israel: "And the LORD directed me at that time to teach you the decrees and laws you are to follow in the land that you are crossing the Jordan to possess" (4 v 14). What Moses calls here "the decrees and laws" are all the other laws.

The purpose of all these laws is to shape a people who will live in harmony with God and at peace with one another, and govern God's world properly. That is to say, they are to shape a people who will remake a broken world. It is helpful to begin to flesh this out by considering briefly the great principles of the Ten Commandments one by one (Exodus 20 v 1-17; Deuteronomy 5 v 6-21).

1. *Only one God:* In a world of many gods, they are to love the God who is One with undivided loyalty. This alone can unite society in joyful true worship.

2. *No idols:* In a world that loves to reshape god in our own image (what I think God ought to be like), they are to worship him only as he has revealed himself. This will prevent the terrible divisiveness of human religion inventing god in all sorts of different human images (and then fighting over which of our images is right).

3. *Honouring the name of God:* In a world that takes God very lightly, they are to honour his "name", that is his revealed character, treating him with reverence. This is the antidote to the pride of Babel.

4. *Sabbath rest:* In an anxious and driven world which prides itself on working 24/7 and cannot risk resting (or letting others rest) they are to rejoice in rhythms of work and rest, trusting in the sufficiency of God so that their prosperity does not depend entirely on them. This will enable them to create a society which is generous in allowing others to rest (see especially the way Moses preaches this commandment in Deuteronomy 5 v 12-15).

5. *Honouring parents:* The command to honour parents stands in the Ten Commandments as a shorthand for respecting all the God-given structures of human authority, since the family is the core and foundation of those structures. To respect authority will prevent society disintegrating into anarchy and chaos, which is why it comes with the promise ("that you may live long in the land") (Exodus 20 v 12; see also Ephesians 6 v 2-3).

6. *No murder:* In a world full of hatred and anger, they are to learn to shun any behaviour that harms or desires to harm another human being. Instead they are to love their

neighbours as themselves (Leviticus 19 v 18).

7. *No adultery:* In an unfaithful world, they are to learn to value sexual faithfulness in the covenant of marriage, and to flee from sexual intimacy in all other contexts. Their society will then be saved from the miserable jealousies and discontent of sexual chaos.

8. *No stealing:* In an unjust world, they are to learn to hate stealing and unjust business dealings. Instead, they are to learn to love generosity, to work that they may have something to share and give, because they know the God who richly gives us all things to enjoy (Ephesians 4 v 28 and 1 Timothy 6 v 17).

9. *No false witness:* In a deceitful world they are to hate false witness, which means lying for our gain and another's harm. They are to love truth, because they know the God who is faithful and true.

10. *No covetousness:* In a self-obsessed world, they are to learn to hate greed and covetousness because they are learning to trust the God who has said, "Never will I leave you; never will I forsake you" (Hebrews 13 v 5). In this way their society can be harmonious and preserved from the miseries of envious covetousness, always looking over our shoulders to see what kind of husband or wife, what kind of job, what kind of house, what kind of holidays and leisure, other people have got.

Only an assembly shaped by this good law will live together in harmony. This law alone is the relational pattern that makes for peace. A society shaped by these principles will live together in peace and not be scattered by strife: it will remake a broken world.

*E. If we shape our own gods we will go back to Babel*
Moses sets before the assembly a simple but very deep choice: either they are shaped by the voice of God and stay gathered, or they shape themselves any way they want and will end up scattered. The great burden of his sermon in Deuteronomy 4 is to warn them of the disastrous results of idolatry.

> You saw no form of any kind the day the LORD spoke to you at Horeb out of the fire. *Therefore watch yourselves very carefully, so that you do not become corrupt and make for yourselves an idol*, an image of any shape, whether formed like a man or a woman, or like any animal on earth or any bird that flies in the air, or like any creature that moves along the ground or any fish in the waters below. And when you look up to the sky and see the sun, the moon and the stars—all the heavenly array—do not be enticed into bowing down to them. (Deuteronomy 4 v 15-19)

To make an idol was precisely what they had done at Sinai. While Moses was up the mountain, we read:

> When the people saw that Moses was so long in coming down from the mountain, they gathered [assembled] round Aaron and said, "Come, make us gods who will go before us." (Exodus 32 v 1)

And so the golden calf was made, shaped by Aaron to reflect the kind of religion they wanted, which was pretty much the same kind of human-centred religion of all the peoples round about, god in the shape we want god to be.

However, they are not to imagine that they can shape and mould God into their own likeness, to make an idol in the shape they want. Either the assembly is shaped by the word of God spoken to them from above, from outside their own hearts and imaginations, or it will be shaped by the desires and imaginations of their own hearts. The broken world will not be remade by human beings gathering together by their own initiative and deciding what they think God ought to be like, for then he will always be a pale reflection of their own culture, and thus always in conflict with other humanly-shaped gods from other cultures. It will only be remade by the sovereign word of God preached to them from outside, over which they have no control and to which they must submit.

For years in my Christian life I thought idolatry in the Bible was what the appendix is in the human body—a relict of some bygone age when no doubt it had a purpose, but not now; leave it out and you won't miss it. There are many evils in the world of which I need to beware, from which I need to guard myself, but surely idolatry is so laughable that I am safe from *that*, I thought. There is an old hymn which begins, "From Greenland's icy mountains, From India's coral strand…" It is about the moral darkness of the rest of the world, in which, in the words of verse two, "The heathen, in his blindness, bows down to wood and stone". But not us! Some time ago, I read in the paper a sculptor in Thailand had added a gold-plated statue of David Beckham to a Buddhist temple in Bangkok, alongside various other minor deities. And of course we laugh. "How absurd!" we say.

In his autobiography *Father and Son*, the nineteenth-century writer Edmund Gosse describes an experiment he carried out as a six-year-old. He had heard his godly parents speak of the terrible sin of idolatry; he asked his father what this was and was told that idolatry consisted in praying to any one or anything but God alone. "Wood and stone were particularly liable to be bowed down to by the heathen in their blindness". Being assured by his father that this sin made God very angry, and that God would signify his anger, the rebellious boy determined to try an experiment.

> I determined ... to test the matter for myself, and one morning, when both my parents were safely out of the house, I prepared for the great act of heresy. I was in the morning-room on the ground-floor, where, with much labour, I hoisted a small chair on to the table close to the window.
>
> My heart was now beating as if it would leap out of my side, but I pursued my experiment. I knelt down on the carpet in front of the table, and looking up I said my daily prayer in a loud voice, only substituting the address "O Chair!" for the habitual one.
>
> Having carried this act of idolatry safely through, I waited to see what would happen. It was a fine day, and I gazed up at the slip of white sky above the houses opposite, and expected something to appear in it. God would certainly exhibit his anger in some terrible form, and would chastise my impious and wilful action... [but nothing happens, and he concludes] I had committed idolatry, flagrantly and deliberately, and God did not care.[35]

But it's such a trivial mistake. Edmund Gosse was an idolater, but not in the way he considered here. He assumed that idolatry was an outward action. And yet the Bible makes clear that idolatry is a matter of the heart. The physical bowing down to an image of wood or stone is but one symptom of the disease of the heart. In two of his letters Paul speaks of greed or covetousness as being idolatry (Ephesians 5 v 5; Colossians 3 v 5). At the end of his first letter John suddenly—

out of the blue it seems—ends with the stark words, "Dear children, keep yourselves from idols"—full stop, end of letter (1 John 5 v 21). So what is idolatry, if it is not just the physical making of an image of a god? In his letter to the church in Rome, Paul says that idolatry means to exchange the truth about God for a lie and to give our worship to things that have been made, rather than to the one creator God (Romans 1 v 23-25). The point about idolatry is this. You and I—and the animals and birds and so on—are created. God is the creator. He made us; we did not make him. He made us human beings in his image, to be like him.

To be an idolater is to turn it upside down, to exchange the creator for the created. So that I—as a created being—put myself in the place of the creator and make for myself a god fashioned in my image, created and shaped by me, chosen by me, so that this is the god of my shaping and my choosing. So although I claim to worship it, in fact it is me who is firmly in control. For if I choose to reshape my god, who is to stop me? I made it; I can remake it. He, she or it is my project, my ambition, my decision.

Human beings are made to worship. We must bow down and serve some god, some cause, some project or some reason for living; we've got to have someone or something to serve; otherwise we'll just roll over on our backs and stick our feet in the air like a dead beetle! As Martin Luther said, "If a man will not have God, he must have his idols". We create our idols all the time when we will not worship God. The Reformer John Calvin said, "the human heart is a factory of idols"; we're always creating new models. It may be a new form of greed. It may be an obsession with success in my career. It may be I make my family into an idol, so that feathering my nest and building up my little nuclear family becomes my big goal, and all my time and all my money is poured into this little family, and woe betide anybody who suggests I might have wider obligations in God's world. We make many idols.

The point at Sinai is not that the Lord was invisible whereas idols are visible. It is not that the Lord is spiritual whereas idols are physical. No, it is that idols are visible but the Lord was *audible*. The difference is profound, because it is the difference of who is in control. *You see,* says Moses, *we saw no form: we do not know what God looks like, we do not know his shape.* So if we make a shape or image it will tell you everything about us and our desires and nothing about God and his character.

But when God speaks it is different: for what he says is not an echo of what is in my heart. He does not rubber-stamp my longings when he speaks. I do not choose what he says. He does not speak in the misquoted "still small voice" inside me, for this so-called voice is a subjective creation of my own complex psyche.[36] No, he speaks objectively in words that come to you and me from outside ourselves. He is in control. He speaks and my duty is to hear and obey. I may or may not find what he says congenial or comfortable, but he speaks.

Let me share with you an analogy which I think helps to make this distinction clear. In his very personal testimony, *A Grief Observed*, C.S. Lewis speaks of what it is to live on after the death of his beloved wife. One of the things he says—and I think this is very profound—is about memory. He speaks of the shallow way people say, "She will live forever in your memory". But he points out that this is utter rubbish. "*Live?* That is exactly what she won't do." And the reason she won't live in his memory is that in his memory she is an image who will do whatever he wants. A remembered image "will smile or frown, be tender, gay, ribald, or argumentative just as your mood demands. It is a puppet of which you hold the strings." But in life she had not been like that. She was another and she chose whether to smile or frown, and so on.[37]

The opposite of idolatry is true worship. The living God is *other* to us. He lives, he speaks, he chooses, he acts, and we respond. By contrast, an idol is an image which does our bidding. That's why real worship is so dangerous: to gather around the word of God and to take seriously what the living God says objectively to us—it's a dangerous adventure. It is possible to go through all the motions of Christian religion and be an idolater, because the so-called "God" we say we worship is actually made in our image—he fits into our tramlines, our box, and does just what we expect him to do. This is why it is so important, says Moses, to submit to his word, for the people of God to be gathered in expectancy under the word of God.

Moses goes on in Deuteronomy 4 to spell out why idolatry matters so deeply. The main thrust of verses 20-24 is the jealousy of God. God is a jealous lover who absolutely insists that his beloved should be his and his alone. This is a good jealousy. It is the jealousy any married person ought to feel, and God feels it for his people, who are his bride. The Covenant is the binding obligation of exclusive mutual love and loyalty.

Idolatry is playing with fire. God's jealous love is like a holy fire which burns with settled and furious anger against infidelity. We must bow down and worship him alone. Idolatry matters because it is a breach of trust. It is infidelity. It is terribly serious. It leads to helpless scattering.

> After you have had children and grandchildren and have lived in the land a long time—if you then become corrupt

and make any kind of idol, doing evil in the eyes of the LORD your God and arousing his anger, I call the heavens and the earth as witnesses against you this day that you will quickly perish from the land that you are crossing the Jordan to possess. You will not live there long but will certainly be destroyed. *The LORD will scatter you* among the peoples, and only a few of you will survive among the nations to which the LORD will drive you. There you will worship man-made gods of wood and stone, which cannot see or hear or eat or smell.

(Deuteronomy 4 v 25-28)

An idolatrous people ends up corrupt, scattered, and defeated. They cry out to the gods they have shaped, and find that those gods have no eyes, ears or power to help them. The whole problem with an idol is that because I made it, it has no power beyond me to help me when I am in need. Idolatry is such a cruel delusion. It is all about image: an idol is like a marketing brand. Like a brand, an idol is very vulnerable to being shown up when it comes face to face with reality. There was a famous advertising copywriter in the 1920s called Helen Woodward who warned anyone writing an advertisement *not* to visit the factory in which the product was made. For, she said, "when you know the truth about anything, the real inner truth—it is very hard to write the surface fluff which sells it."[38] When idolatry comes face to face with suffering and pain it is shown up for the dead sham that it is. No one facing a terminal illness says, "I wish I had passed more exams, I wish I had spent more hours in the office, I wish I had got more promotions, I wish I had earned more money, I wish I had followed the lifestyle magazines more slavishly, I wish I had owned more…"

Some years ago the little toddler Jamie Bulger was abducted and murdered by two ten-year-old boys in Liverpool. The crime provoked widespread questioning about our society. One national newspaper proclaimed in a headline, "All our gods have failed". That was true. When a society worships success, technology, power or wealth, and then finds moral decay in its midst, to whom can we turn? Will our careers save us? Will our wealth save us? Can technology bring moral order out of moral decay? All those gods have failed and will always fail.

One of the main lessons we learn from Sinai is that gathering is only possible when God does it, and when the people who are gathered submit to the word of God and allow their relationships to be shaped by it. Whenever we shape gods to suit our own desires we end up scattered, back at Babel.

The problem was that ancient Israel was at heart still a nation of idolaters, and Moses knew it. The sad irony is that they continued to shape their own gods—and they did end up back in Babel.

*F. The Sinai church is an assembly at a distance*
So far in our study of Sinai we have not dwelt on one of the most striking features of this assembly. It may be a wonderful thing to see the first God-called church east of Eden, but it has a very different feel from those wonderful days in the garden before Adam's disobedience.

There, the Lord walked in the garden and spoke with his gardeners as with his friends. Here, he descends from heaven to the top of the mountain in fire, darkness, gloom and storm, speaking words so terrifying the people begged him to stop and let Moses be their mediator and God's spokesman. If even an animal touched the mountain while God was on the top of it, it had to be killed from a distance by arrows or stoning:

anyone who touched a creature that had touched the sacred mountain would be killed.

The writer of the New Testament letter to the Hebrews (i.e. to Jewish Christians) describes that day as coming…

> … to a mountain that can be touched [that is, a darkness so thick you could metaphorically touch it] and that is burning with fire; to darkness, gloom and storm; to a trumpet blast or to such a voice speaking words that those who heard it begged that no further word be spoken to them, because they could not bear what was commanded: "If even an animal touches the mountain, it must be stoned to death." The sight was so terrifying that Moses said, "I am trembling with fear."
>
> (Hebrews 12 v 18-21)

What a frightening assembly, what a terrifying church to come to! It was not an assembly for access to God, but rather an assembly in which they had to keep their distance from God. This paradox signals to us that the gateway into Eden is still guarded by the cherubim and flaming sword (Genesis 3 v 24). These angels were like God's bouncers, preventing human beings from re-entering Eden. It is going to be no light matter to remake a broken world, for human beings with rebellious hearts will be burned up by the fire of God's holiness if they come into his presence. In words echoed in the New Testament, Moses says to them that, "the LORD your God is a consuming fire, a jealous God" (Deuteronomy 4 v 24; Hebrews 12 v 29). To say he is "a jealous God" simply means he must have our complete and wholehearted loyalty: we cannot "two-time" God by having an affair with other gods, and still live; he is the all or nothing God. That is the inevitable consequence of God being One. He cannot just stand down his bouncers, say he's changed his mind and feels he's been a bit tough on Adam and Eve, and just let us back into the garden. The moral coherence of the universe would disintegrate if he did that without our rebellion being atoned for.

And yet unless we are brought back into his presence we cannot live in harmony with one another or with the created order. So what is to be done? This tension lies beneath that great day at Sinai, and all the law given then. Moses' sermon in Deuteronomy 4 ends not with human failure but with God's promise, the promise of a remade world. Looking ahead to days of exile, Moses concludes:

> When you are in distress and all these things have hap-
> pened to you, then in later days you will return to the
> LORD your God and obey him. For the LORD your God
> is a merciful God; he will not abandon or destroy you
> or forget the covenant with your ancestors, which he
> confirmed to them by oath. (Deuteronomy 4 v 30-31)

It is a relief to know the letter to the Hebrews, in the passage quoted above, says that Christian people have *not* come to Mount Sinai in our churches (Hebrews 12 v 18)! So although we learn important lessons about submission to the word of God, thank God that there are some wonderful differences between the Sinai church and church today.

## Questions for Discussion

1. Review what happened between Babel and Sinai. In what ways had God's promise of remaking a broken world begun, and in what ways had it not yet?

2. What new thing happened at Sinai?

3. Think carefully about your local church meetings. In what ways is the life of your local church shaped and driven by listening to the voice of God through the Bible?

4. How do you think we shape God to be the way we would like him to be? In particular, how can we find ourselves using the Bible to make God seem the way we would like him to be?

5. Are there projects or people in church life that become so important to us that we are in danger of making them into idols? How can we avoid this?

# FOUR

# Jerusalem: Gathered Under the King

We ended the last chapter by noting the letter to the Hebrews says that Christians have *not* come to Mount Sinai when they assemble. This is why we drew lines from only some of the pattern of Sinai to the church, but not all. The writer goes on to say, "But you *have* come to Mount Zion, to ... the heavenly Jerusalem" (Hebrews 12 v 22). He is speaking in symbolic terms, and we shall see in Chapter 9 what he means by "the heavenly Jerusalem". To help us understand the heavenly Jerusalem, we need first to see the significance of the earthly Jerusalem in Old Testament times.

### From Sinai to Jerusalem

The journey from Sinai to Jerusalem took centuries. First there was a 40-year wandering in the desert (Numbers 10 v 11 – 36 v 13, summarised by Moses in Deuteronomy 1 v 19 – 3 v 29). Then the book of Deuteronomy records Moses' final preaching to the people on the edge of the Promised Land. The book of Joshua records the invasion and settlement of the land. The book of Judges recounts how Israel was governed (or "judged") for many years by a strange sequence of Spirit-anointed leaders raised up by God. Then in 1 Samuel we read the story of how first Saul and then David are made king over Israel. It is not until 2 Samuel 5 v 6-9 that David conquers Jerusalem.

## Jerusalem

Jerusalem became enormously significant for the assembly of the people of God. We find its meaning especially celebrated in some of the psalms. I shall take Psalm 122 to give us four of the most important meanings of Jerusalem.

I rejoiced with those who said to me,
    "Let us go to the house of the Lord."
Our feet are standing
    in your gates, Jerusalem.

Jerusalem is built like a city
    that is closely compacted together.
That is where the tribes go up—
    the tribes of the Lord—
to praise the name of the Lord
    according to the statute given to Israel.
There stand the thrones for judgment,
    the thrones of the house of David.

Pray for the peace of Jerusalem:
    "May those who love you be secure.
May there be peace within your walls
    and security within your citadels."
For the sake of my family and friends,
    I will say, "Peace be within you."
For the sake of the house of the Lord our God,
    I will seek your prosperity.

Each of Psalms 120 to 134 is headed "A Song of Ascents". The psalms in this collection are to be sung going "up" to Jerusalem, probably by pilgrims going up for the great Jewish festivals like Passover or Tabernacles. These were the times of "sacred assembly" when all Israel gathered in Jerusalem (Leviticus 23 v 4). They were not going "up" because Jerusalem is an especially high mountain. It isn't all that high. Although it is in a hilly region, even the Mount of Olives is higher, and one of this same collection of psalms speaks of the mountains surrounding Jerusalem (Psalm 125 v 2)! No, they spoke of going "up" because Jerusalem was important. In a similar way, in England we sometimes speak about going "up" to London, because London is our capital city. In Old Testament terms, you could start your journey on the top of Mount Everest, but if you were going to Jerusalem, you had to go "up": it was the most important place on earth. We shall see why.

There seems to be something of a progression in the first three psalms of the collection. Psalm 120 sings of the misery of living in a broken world. "Too long," sings the psalmist, "have I lived among those who hate peace" (v 6). He longs for peace, and in Psalm 121 he begins his journey up to Jerusalem, the city of peace; the Hebrew *salem* comes from "shalom" meaning "peace" (rather like the Arabic *salaam*). Jerusalem was the place on earth where peace was to be found. This is why the psalmist rejoices at the start of Psalm 122 when his friends suggest going up to Jerusalem on pilgrimage. This psalm is about the place of peace that speaks of the remaking of a world at war.

In verses 1-5 he rejoices in four characteristics of Jerusalem: a "house" (v 1), a "city" (v 3), united "tribes" (v 4) and "thrones" (v 5). Each of these will unlock a truth about the meaning of

Old Testament Jerusalem: they speak of access, security, unity and government. We shall consider them in turn.

*A. Access: Jerusalem is where God lives on earth*

The psalm is bracketed by references to "the house of the LORD" (v 1, 9); this means the Temple, where God (in Old Testament symbolism) lived on earth. We saw in Chapter 1 that when Adam and Eve were expelled from the Garden of Eden a rift occurred between heaven and earth. From that time on the harmony of the universe was disrupted. Heaven became God's space *as opposed to* our human space, and "earth" became the space (the material space-time universe) where God no longer lived in a direct relational way. But heaven began very soon to reinvade earth, to create meeting points—places and ways in which some kind of access to heaven might be enjoyed by the believer on earth.[39] The various altars erected by Abraham, Isaac and Jacob were such meeting places, and especially the altar on Mount Moriah where Abraham sacrificed the substitute ram in place of Isaac on the site where, centuries later, Solomon built the Temple (Genesis 22 v 1-19; 2 Chronicles 3 v 1). So was the place where Jacob had a dream of a ladder reaching from earth to heaven (Genesis 28 v 10-22). In the wilderness between Sinai and the Promised Land, the Tabernacle (or Tent) fulfilled this role (Exodus 25–40). In the Tabernacle was the special box (the Ark of the Covenant) containing the two stone tablets inscribed with the Ten Commandments; this was pictured as being the "footstool" under God's throne, the place where God placed his feet on earth.[40] Finally, the mobile Tabernacle was replaced by Solomon's Temple (1 Kings 5–8).

The Tabernacle and the Temple were designed to echo the Garden of Eden in a number of ways.[41] Just as God "walked" in the garden, so he "walks" among his people in the Tabernacle and Temple.[42] The garden was entered from the East and guarded by cherubim; in the same way, the Tabernacle and Temple were entered from the East and guarded by cherubim.[43] Just as the garden is a source of a life-giving river, so Ezekiel's Temple vision has a life-giving river flowing out of the Temple.[44] The Tabernacle contained a branched lampstand (the Menorah) and the Temple had tree decorations on its pillars, both of which may symbolise the Tree of Life.[45] In these and other ways the Tabernacle and Temple were meant at least to hint that access might one day be possible back into the Garden of Eden.

The reason sinful people could come close to a holy God is this was the place of sacrifice. The utterly fair but steady and hot anger of God against sinners was poured out, in symbolic form, on an animal sacrifice, so that the sacrifice was burnt up in the place of the worshipper. The sacrifice was (in the technical term) a "propitiation", which means a sacrifice which appeases wrath. In Chapter 6 we shall see this fulfilled at the Cross.

Verse 2 of Psalm 122 is spoken in tones of awe and wonder. How wonderful, he sings, that now at last our feet can stand within the gates of Jerusalem itself! He is amazed to stand within the gates of the city where God lives. He knows he does not deserve it: no one deserves it. He stands there by grace. He feels the wonder of the presence of God in the city of peace. This is the place that God loves. The same sense of wonder is evident in Psalm 87, with its vision that from all over the world people will see no higher privilege than to have been "born" in Zion, a vivid way of speaking of their identity as children of Zion, and therefore children of God. We find a deep sense of longing to be in Zion also in Psalm 84, where the singers yearn and faint with longing, crying out to be in the presence of the living

God: they can hardly wait until they, with other pilgrims, appear before God in Zion (v 1, 2, 7).

Having said all this, we must remember the access given to the immediate presence of God was still very limited. Just as at Sinai only Moses (or Moses with Aaron and the elders) could go onto the mountain, so in the Temple only the priests could go in, and only the High Priest into the Holy of Holies, and that only once a year and with great care. Nevertheless, there is a sense of wonder that God dwells among his people. The Tabernacle at the centre of the camp in the wilderness, and the Temple at the heart of Jerusalem, foreshadowed the day in the future of which Hebrews 12 speaks, when all the people of God have unconstrained access to God because of Jesus.

For our theme of scattering and gathering, here is a significant point to note: Israel are gathered in Jerusalem *around the presence of God* to show they can only be gathered to one another when they are *first gathered to God.*

*B. Security: Jerusalem is the only truly safe place on earth*
In Psalm 122 v 3 the psalmist looks round at Jerusalem and exclaims:

Jerusalem is built like a city
    that is closely compacted together.

Our translation makes it sound a bit like Singapore, as though "closely compacted together" meant having a high housing density! The psalmist does not mean this at all. He means it is a solid city, with no fractures in its walls, no weaknesses in its defences, and not divided against itself. It is not like Berlin from the 1950s to the 1980s, with a dividing wall down the middle. He looks around and sees Jerusalem as a rock-solid secure place in an insecure world: it is impregnable.

*Look around,* he sings, *at this safe place, this solid place, this city with foundations and walls, this place that cannot be attacked or shaken. This is a place of solidity, of glory, of weight, of substance, of great stone buildings and fine stone walls. I feel safe here inside these gates.*

Some years ago when I was visiting Japan there was a great scandal breaking out. Because Japan suffers frequent earthquakes, the cities have strict building regulations governing the earthquake-proofing of high-rise buildings. A prominent architect in Tokyo was arrested and charged with falsifying the earthquake-proofing certificates for a number of these buildings. If this was true, it was obviously very serious. Buildings that appeared secure were actually likely to fall down when the earthquake came. It is a picture of the false security offered by idols. A "career ladder" invites us to get on the first rung and climb up and up and up, feeling safe inside that "building": the reality is if we trust our careers for security, when the shocks of God's judgment storms come, we will find the earthquake-proofing we had been promised was a fraud.

But Jerusalem in Old Testament symbolism is the only really safe place on earth. This sense of security, that the people of God can safely assemble here, is apparent in other places. We see this confidence in Psalm 125, another of the Psalms of Ascent: "Those who trust in the LORD are like Mount Zion, which cannot be shaken but endures for ever" (v 1). Psalm 48 is a great celebration of "Mount Zion, the city of the Great King" which is "secure for ever" even though it will be attacked (v 2, 8).

Perhaps the most vivid Old Testament drama of the security of Jerusalem happened when the Assyrian King Sennacherib attacked and surrounded it during the reign of King Hezekiah. The people of God were assembled, even huddled, together within the besieged walls that must have seemed so fragile and vulnerable. But God wonderfully protected his city so they could even laugh with scorn at their attacker (2 Kings 18–19; see especially 19 v 21). To assemble in the place where God lives is to gather in safety.

The hymn writer John Newton (the author of "Amazing Grace") expressed this wonderfully in his great hymn:

Glorious things of thee are spoken,
Zion, city of our God.
He, whose word cannot be broken,
Form'd thee for his own abode:
On the Rock of Ages founded,
What can shake thy sure repose?
With salvation's walls surrounded,
Thou may'st smile at all thy foes.

*C. Harmony: Jerusalem is the only place where warring tribes unite*
The third thing about Jerusalem that makes the psalmist rejoice (and this lies close to the heart of our theme of gathering) is in verse 4. Jerusalem is the place where the usually quarrelling tribes of Israel unite in worship.

That is where the tribes go up—
    the tribes of the LORD—
to praise the name of the LORD
    according to the statute given to Israel.

Jerusalem is the only place where warring tribes can be brought together in peace. On the journey from Sinai to Jerusalem, Israel was just as divided and fractious as the rest of the human race. This is particularly seen in the tensions between the tribes. Much of Joshua is taken up with allocating sections of the conquered land to the different tribes

(Joshua 13–21). This includes some territory to the east of the Jordan, which had been conquered first and was allocated to the tribes of Reuben and Gad, and the half-tribe of Manasseh. We come very close to a civil war between these two and a half tribes and the rest in Joshua 22. Tribal tensions are never far below the surface in Judges. We see these tensions, for example, when the Ephraimites are angry with Gideon, who is from Manasseh, or when the Ephraimites (again!) are angry with Jephthah the Gileadite (Judges 8 v 1; 6 v 15; 11 v 1; 12 v 1). Judges ends with the whole tribe of Benjamin being threatened with genocide by the other tribes (Judges 20–21)! The history of Israel is a history of tribal conflict. We continue to see this later in Israel's history with the conflicts between Saul's followers in the tribe of Benjamin and David's from the tribe of Judah, and in the civil war that followed Solomon's death.

The tribes of Israel are not naturally united: far from it. By nature they are as disunited as the original sons of Jacob from whom they were descended. They unite only when they agree to "go up", and when they go up, they then bow down in worship, adoration and praise, not of themselves but of the God who has redeemed them. When they seek to "climb up" to their own towers like Babel, they end up at war and scattered.

There are actually only two options for human society: true worship and war. Only true worship humbles human pride. False worship and war go together, because false worship exalts the worshipper, who is really only worshipping an idol of their creation or imagination. Only in worship of the true God will people be brought so low that our aspirations to greatness will be removed, and our empire-building plans abandoned. Only in true worship will we live together in weakness and without pretensions.

The psalmist rejoices to see men and women from different tribes going up with him to Jerusalem to worship and praise God together. He loves to see fellow believers humbled together under the mighty hand of God to offer praise to the Redeemer God rather than seeking praise for themselves.

The theme of "assembly" is one of the ways the psalms often speak of Jerusalem. "Praise God in the great congregation; praise the LORD in the assembly of Israel" (Psalm 68 v 26).[46] Worship and praise are the key to successful gathering of naturally warring tribes. The psalmist feels the wonder of united thanksgiving in the city of peace.

### D. Government: Jerusalem is the place from which God's king rules the world

The fourth reason the psalmist rejoices to be in Jerusalem is in Psalm 122 v 5. Jerusalem is the place from which God's anointed king rules.

> There stand the thrones for judgment,
> the thrones of the house of David.

One of the reasons Israelites went on pilgrimage to Jerusalem was to have their legal business attended to by the highest courts in the land. This was the place where the judges sat (hence the plural "thrones"). We might speak of going to where the Supreme Court or the High Court sits. Those judges were just if—and only if—they served a just king.

The Old Testament equivalent of a coronation was an anointing. Instead of placing a crown on the king's head, you poured oil over him (see, for example, the anointing of David in 1 Samuel 16 v 1-13). He became the "anointed one", for which the Hebrew word is "Messiah" and the Greek word "Christ". The psalmist is glad to go to Jerusalem because that is where God's anointed one, God's king, God's Messiah, God's Christ, rules with justice.

To understand why the psalmist is so glad, we need to go back in Israel's history to the time before they were ruled by God's anointed king. Without a strong king, a people will end up scattered.

One way of looking at gathering and scattering is in terms of whose side we are on in a war. It is common imagery to speak of a leader assembling troops for battle, and a defeated army being scattered.[47] Sometimes the Old Testament speaks of the LORD as a warrior leading his people to victory. They often spoke of God's enemies being scattered.[48] Of course, this is a double-edged truth. It means if my enemies are God's enemies, my enemies will be scattered: but it also means if I worship idols, then I will be among the scattered, for I will have lined myself up with God's enemies. I cannot have it both ways, living without God and expecting to stay gathered in peace.

To be saved is to be gathered together with the whole people of God under God's leader; I cannot be saved as an individual without being gathered to God's people. We see this clearly in the climax of a great prayer King David later gave to the people: "*Save* us, God our Saviour; *gather* us and deliver us from the nations"; to be saved is to be gathered out of the nations into the presence of God (1 Chronicles 16 v 35).

This military use of the gathering and scattering imagery raises the question of the human leadership of the people of God. Who is going to be God's delegated instrument to gather the people for victory and stop them being scattered to the four winds?

They certainly needed such a leader. Tribal tensions and strife were particularly bad during the period of the "Judges". In many ways judges like Gideon, Samson and Jephthah seem more like local tribal warlords than leaders of all Israel. The writer of Judges leaves us in no doubt that the problem is that they have no overall God-given leader. The final chapters of Judges paint a terrible picture of social breakdown (Judges 17–21). This is punctuated four times by a refrain which makes the cause clear:

> In those days Israel had no king; everyone did
> as they saw fit. (17 v 6)
> In those days Israel had no king. (18 v 1)
> In those days Israel had no king. (19 v 1)
> In those days Israel had no king; everyone did
> as they saw fit. (21 v 25)

The point is that scattering is not an unusual phenomenon in Israel: it is the default state of Israel, as it is the default state of every human society, following the pattern of Babel. If Israel is to be united, they must be given a king. So when we begin the books of Samuel the question in our minds is, "Will Israel have a king, and if so, what sort of king?" That question is answered when, after a long story, David becomes king.[49] One of the very first things he did was to conquer Jerusalem, "the fortress of Zion" which he renamed "the city of David" (2 Samuel 5 v 6-9).

David was a shepherd, or "pastor". From the time of David onwards there was a particularly strong association between kingship and shepherding. A shepherd in those cultures was the leader and protector of his flock. Without his protection the flock would be scattered by wolves, "harassed and helpless, like sheep without a shepherd", "scattered because there was no shepherd" (Matthew 9 v 36; Ezekiel 34 v 5). A shepherd gathers his flock together in safety (see, for example, 2 Samuel 7 v 5-16).

## Old Testament Jerusalem and the Jerusalem of Promise

So in Psalm 122 v 1-5, the psalmist looks around Jerusalem with the eyes of faith. He sees the place on earth which combines the presence of God, the security of the people of God, the harmonious gathering of the people of God and the just government of God's Christ. These four themes are closely connected. The reasons Jerusalem is so safe and peaceful are the presence of God and the rule of God's Christ. Because God is there in the Temple and rules his people by his king, Jerusalem is a place of harmony and security. Stable and lasting gathering is possible only in the presence of God under the government of God's king.

Jerusalem signifies all this, and our pilgrim sees all this with the eyes of faith. For the moment he looks around at the actual historical Jerusalem, and he knows he will be sadly disappointed. Instead of being a place of security, all too often it was a place where the weak were oppressed. Instead of being a place of unity, all too often it was a place of massive social inequality. Instead of being a place where justice was done, all too often it was just the opposite. For example, in Isaiah's day, we read that God "looked [in Jerusalem] for justice, but saw bloodshed; for righteousness, but heard cries of distress" (Isaiah 5 v 7).

It is because the real Old Testament Jerusalem fell far short of the Jerusalem of promise that the psalmist ends with exhorting us to pray that the city called the "city of peace" will live up to its name:

Pray for the peace of Jerusalem:
  "May those who love you be secure.
May there be peace within your walls

and security within your citadels."
For the sake of my family and friends,
    I will say, "Peace be within you."
For the sake of the house of the LORD our God,
    I will seek your prosperity. (Psalm 122 v 6-9)

All through the disappointments of Israel's history the promise kept being repeated—that one day there would be a Jerusalem that really lived up to its name. Here is one of the most famous of those prophecies:

This is what Isaiah son of Amoz saw concerning Judah and Jerusalem:

In the last days
the mountain of the LORD's temple will be established
    as the highest of the mountains;
it will be exalted above the hills,
    all nations will stream to it.

Many peoples will come and say,
"Come, let us go up to the mountain of the LORD,
    to the temple of the God of Jacob.
He will teach us his ways,
    so that we may walk in his paths."
The law will go out from Zion,
    the word of the LORD from Jerusalem.
He will judge between the nations
    and will settle disputes for many peoples.
They will beat their swords into ploughshares
    and their spears into pruning hooks.
Nation will not take up sword against nation,
    nor will they train for war any more.
(Isaiah 2 v 1-4, substantially repeated in Micah 4 v 1-3)

Here, in vision, is a city to which we must indeed go "up", for it is now "established as the highest of the mountains ... exalted above the hills". The whole world will gather there ("all nations will stream to it"—a wonderful picture of a fragmented world being reassembled in Jerusalem). They go there because this is the place from which God's instruction ("the law ... the word of the LORD," v 3) goes out from Zion. It is the place where just judgment will at last be done (v 4), disputes settled, wars ended and harmony established on earth at last. This is the significance of Jerusalem in Bible language.

## Where is Jerusalem today?

This will be a good point in our journey to pause and ask, "Where is Jerusalem today?" That may seem a silly question, but it is not. We have seen that Jerusalem in Bible language was not only a physical place but also meant something, and what it meant did not correspond with what it was actually like on the ground. When we read the language of Jerusalem in our Bibles today, what should we be thinking about? What does the writer of the letter to the Hebrews mean by saying to Christian people that when they assemble for church they, "have come to Mount Zion, to ... the heavenly Jerusalem" (Hebrews 12 v 22)?

Here are four pointers which will anticipate some themes we shall explore later in our Bible tour. The first is a necessary negative. The second, third and fourth are positive.

### 1. "Jerusalem" is not in the Middle East

Under the Old Covenant, in Old Testament times, Jerusalem was quite simply and literally a place, a city. You could find it on a map. You can find where it *was*, in a Bible atlas. But Jerusalem in a Bible atlas, or Jerusalem the capital of the state of Israel, is not the same as Jerusalem in New Covenant Bible significance. When today under the New Covenant we speak of Jerusalem, we are not speaking of travelling to the Middle East. If we were, then Christianity would be an elite religion in which those who could afford the tours were more privileged than poor Christians who could not. But Christianity is the very opposite of an elite religion.

The reason Jerusalem now does not have the significance of Jerusalem then is very simple: what made Jerusalem significant then was the Temple, the place on earth where God dwelt. But in AD 70 the Temple was destroyed. Indeed the New Testament speaks sadly of the physical Jerusalem after Jesus: it even calls it the place of judgment, the place of spiritual slavery (Galatians 4 v 25).

All through Israel's history there was this tension between Jerusalem as spoken of in faith, and the historical reality. Gradually, they began to grasp that the physical Jerusalem, like everything else in the Old Covenant, was but a shadow pointing forward to a substantial reality to be revealed later.

### 2. "Jerusalem" is fulfilled in the Lord Jesus Christ

Supremely, Jerusalem meant what the Temple meant: the presence of God on earth, the one place on earth where human beings could meet God without being burnt alive.

But 2000 years ago one who is greater than the Temple stood on earth (Matthew 12 v 6). He "made his dwelling among us"— literally "tabernacled among us", fulfilling among us what the Tabernacle had meant in the wilderness (John 1 v 14). Jesus spoke of his body as a "Temple" that would be destroyed and then "rebuilt" in three days (John 2 v 19-22). On the Cross he was the place where sinful human beings can meet with God without being destroyed: all that Jerusalem symbolised is fulfilled in Jesus. He is the place where we meet God, the place where we are secure, the place where squabbling people can unite, and the place where God's king rules on earth.

### 3. "Jerusalem" is foreshadowed in the local church

What Jerusalem means is anticipated now on earth in the local church. Jesus is to be found now on earth where his people gather. They, corporately as local churches, are God's Temple, the place where God dwells among his people by his Spirit (1 Corinthians 3 v 16). (The individual Christian's body is also called a "temple of the Holy Spirit" as an incentive to sexual purity (1 Corinthians 6 v 19), but the major emphasis is corporate rather than individual, as in 2 Corinthians 6 v 16 and Ephesians 2 v 21-22.) They are being built into a spiritual house, a temple, and therefore, by the Spirit of God, the local church is a partial fulfilment of "Jerusalem" (1 Peter 2 v 5). It is a local expression and foretaste, an anticipation, a foreshadowing, a partial but real expression of "Jerusalem" here on earth.

### 4. "Jerusalem" is waiting to come down from heaven to fill the earth

Hebrews 12 speaks of coming to "the heavenly Jerusalem" (v 22). One day the real and final Jerusalem will come down from heaven to earth, and fill the earth, and be the New Creation (Revelation 21 v 2). We shall develop this theme in Chapter 9.

So "Jerusalem" is focused on Jesus, anticipated and partially experienced in the local church, and will be fully and finally experienced in the New Creation.

## What does "Jerusalem" mean for local church life?

Each of the themes of Psalm 122 can be traced forward into the life of a local church. Just as the psalmist grieves and feels the pain of living in a broken world (e.g. Psalm 120), so we ought to be able to long for our local church meetings as God's supernatural antidote to a broken world. They ought to be places where the presence of God is known on earth by his Spirit, where real and lasting security is found in an insecure and dangerous world, where harmony is experienced by "tribes" who would naturally be at war, and where a people commit themselves to being governed in justice by God's Christ through his word. A local church that expresses, albeit partially and imperfectly, something of what Jerusalem promised in the Old Testament, will be God's instrument for remaking a broken world. We shall explore these themes further in Chapter 8.

## Questions for Discussion

1. In what ways have you experienced the "woe is me" of living in a warlike world and being unable to make peace (Psalm 120 v 6)?

2. Review the teaching from Psalm 122. What major features of Jerusalem did we note?

3. Have you experienced in the context of Christian fellowship:
   (a) the joy of knowing we have access together to God in Jesus?
   (b) the assurance of knowing that in Jesus we are secure for ever?
   (c) the surprise and wonder of finding people who would not usually get along together actually beginning to love one another?
   (d) a shared agreement to submit to Jesus Christ as God's king ruling his people by his word the Bible?

4. What should we expect in a local church? How do we cope when our experience is disappointing? How should this sharpen our hope for the New Creation?

# FIVE

# Babylon: Back to Babel

And then it all fell apart. The gathering at Sinai and the regular assemblies in Jerusalem all ended in terrible scatterings. This chapter is themed all around "Babylon", but by "Babylon" I mean the theological idea of "Babylon" and not just the historical city of Babylon. Babylon is a paradoxical "place" in the Bible, as it is the place to which the people of God are scattered. How can you be scattered to a place?! Of course on the map it was a city (now in Iraq), the capital of the Neo-Babylonian empire, and later a significant city in the Persian empire. But in Bible language "Babylon" is a "place" standing for many places, or no fixed place: it is a place defined by where it is not (i.e. Jerusalem) rather than by where it is. To "go to Babylon" is not to assemble in Babylon, but to be scattered to Babylon. It is a place only in the sense that outer space is a place.

## From Jerusalem to Babylon

We now move in overview over a vast sweep of Old Testament history, all the way from the great united kingdom of all Israel under King David and his son King Solomon, to the final scattering in the Babylonian exile in 587 BC. We are going to greatly simplify this sweep of history and look at three significant "scattering events", in each of which the unity of the people of God was broken.

## A. The tearing apart of the kingdom into Israel and Judah

The first fracture happened almost immediately after King Solomon's death. The seeds of division had been sown during Solomon's reign as he imposed slave labour on the Israelites and so broke the law of God. Solomon was not faithful to the LORD and the result, as always, was strife (1 Kings 5 v 13-16; 11 v 1-43). One particular source of trouble was a capable civil servant called Jeroboam, who had a meeting with a prophet called Ahijah. This is what happened:

About that time Jeroboam was going out of Jerusalem, and Ahijah the prophet of Shiloh met him on the way, wearing a new cloak. The two of them were alone out in the country, and Ahijah took hold of the new cloak he was wearing and tore it into twelve pieces. Then he said to Jeroboam, "Take ten pieces for yourself, for this is what the Lord, the God of Israel, says: 'See, I am going to tear the kingdom out of Solomon's hand and give you ten tribes. But for the sake of my servant David and the city of Jerusalem, which I have chosen out of all the tribes of Israel, he will have one tribe. I will do this because they have forsaken me and worshipped Ashtoreth the goddess of the Sidonians, Chemosh the god of the Moabites, and Molek the god of the Ammonites, and have not walked in obedience to me, nor done what is right in my eyes, nor kept my decrees and laws as David, Solomon's father, did.

'But I will not take the whole kingdom out of Solomon's hand; I have made him ruler all the days of his life for the sake of David my servant, whom I chose and who obeyed my commands and decrees. I will take the kingdom from his son's hands and give you ten tribes. I will give one tribe to his son so that David my servant may always have a lamp before me in Jerusalem, the city where I chose to put my Name.'" (1 Kings 11 v 29-36)

Jeroboam's new cloak was dramatically torn into twelve pieces, as a sign that the unity of Israel was going to be torn apart after Solomon's death. Ten tribes would follow Jeroboam and the remaining two (Judah and Benjamin, sometimes spoken of as just one, because Benjamin was so small) would remain in David's dynasty. This happened at the start of the reign of Solomon's son Rehoboam (1 Kings 12).

Israel now became the name, no longer of the whole people of God, but just of the ten tribes in the northern kingdom, with its capital at Samaria. The rest, just two tribes, were named after the bigger of the two, Judah (from which we get our word "Jew"), and continued with kings in David's line and his capital Jerusalem. This terrible event is described as God tearing Israel away from the house of David (2 Kings 17 v 21). From that day onwards the tribes never went unitedly up to Jerusalem to worship. Solomon's unfaithfulness to God led to scattering of the people of God. Harmony is only possible in faithful fellowship with God.

## B. The scattering of the northern kingdom by Assyria
The second scattering event was when the northern kingdom was itself scattered by Assyria. Jeroboam became the first king of an independent Israel. He had been promised by the

prophet Ahijah that if he was faithful to the Lord, he too could found an enduring dynasty. He proved himself the exact opposite of faithful to the Lord, setting up a rival religion.[50] 1 Kings 12 to 2 Kings 17 tells the two interlinking stories of Israel and Judah. The story of the northern kingdom came to an end in the year 729 BC when the inhabitants were deported to various different places by the king of Assyria (2 Kings 17 v 1-6). The territory of the ten northern tribes was resettled by the king of Assyria with a random mixture of peoples, who settled down to an eclectic pick'n'mix of religions; their descendants were the religiously-mixed and despised people later called the Samaritans (as in the parable of the Good Samaritan) (2 Kings 17 v 7-41).

The prophet Hosea spoke to the northern kingdom shortly before this happened. In a terrible acted parable of Israel's unfaithfulness he marries Gomer, an unfaithful wife, and she bears a daughter and a son by other men. Hosea is to call the girl "Lo-Ruhamah", which is the Hebrew for "not loved"; he is to call the boy "Lo-Ammi", the Hebrew for "not my people" (Hosea 1 v 1-9). At the very heart of the disaster that befalls Israel is the fracture in their covenant relationship with the LORD: this is why they are scattered.

## C. The scattering of Judah to Babylon

The final and climactic scattering was the exile of the southern kingdom Judah to Babylon. Judah survived precariously for a little over a century after the northern kingdom had been wiped off the map until in 587 BC the Neo-Babylonian empire, which had succeeded the Assyrian empire as regional superpower, invaded Judah and finally sacked Jerusalem, destroying Solomon's magnificent Temple and taking the people into exile (2 Kings 18–25). It makes terrible reading.

## D. The scattering of the covenant curse

So by these three traumatic scatterings God's wonderful gathering was effectively destroyed. All the hopes that a broken world would be remade through Abraham's family seemed to be dashed. God had promised a remade world: but the paradox was that it was the God who made the promise who did the scattering. Again and again the Bible says that although these scatterings happened through the processes of politics and international affairs, behind these forces lay the determined and deliberate will of God acting in just judgment (the human powers that "scattered Judah, Israel and Jerusalem" are called "horns" in Zechariah 1 v 19).

Right at the start of Israel's life, when God first made a covenant with them, he made it clear if they were unfaithful to him they would be scattered. Moses said this to them repeatedly:

> If you … become corrupt and make any kind of idol, doing evil in the eyes of the LORD your God and arousing his anger … The LORD will scatter you among the peoples. (Deuteronomy 4 v 25-27)

> If you do not obey the LORD your God … the LORD will cause you to be defeated before your enemies. You will come at them from one direction [i.e. as a gathered army] but flee from them in seven [i.e. as a scattered rabble] … Then the LORD will scatter you among all nations, from one end of the earth to the other.
> (Deuteronomy 28 v 15, 25, 64)

Idolatry separates people from the one God who alone can enable them to live in harmony. A community that will not bow before the God who is One is bound to end up scattered, just as the builders of Babel were dispersed.

Retelling the story of the LORD's faithfulness and Israel's unfaithfulness, Psalm 106 recounts that:

Then they despised the pleasant land [i.e. the Promised Land];
    they did not believe his promise.
They grumbled in their tents
    and did not obey the LORD.
So he swore to them with uplifted hand
    that he would make them fall in the wilderness,
make their descendants fall among the nations
    and *scatter* them throughout the lands. (v 24-27)

Psalm 44 laments that, in the exile:

You gave us up to be devoured like sheep
    and have *scattered* us among the nations. (v 11)

Towards the end of Judah's existence, the prophet Jeremiah made himself very unpopular by some forceful preaching of the covenant curses. He often used the language of scattering.

The LORD said, "It is because they have forsaken my law ..." Therefore "... I will *scatter* them among nations that neither they nor their ancestors have known."
                                                    (Jeremiah 9 v 13-16)

The shepherds [that is, Israel's leaders, who ought to have been doing what David was anointed to do] are senseless
    and do not enquire of the LORD;
so they do not prosper
    and all their flock is *scattered*. (10 v 21)

I will *scatter* you like chaff
    driven by the desert wind. (13 v 24)

Like a wind from the east,
> I will *scatter* them before their enemies;
I will show them my back and not my face
> in the day of their disaster. (18 v 17)

Notice how alienation from God ("I will show them my back") leads to being scattered before their enemies.

"Woe to the shepherds who are destroying and *scattering* the sheep of my pasture!" declares the LORD ... "You have *scattered* my flock and driven them away and have not bestowed care on them" (23 v 1-2)

And so, when it happened, Jeremiah could lament:

The LORD himself has *scattered* them;
> he no longer watches over them.

(Lamentations 4 v 16)

Ezekiel says something very similar:

Also with uplifted hand I swore to them in the wilderness that I would *disperse* them among the nations and *scatter* them throughout the countries, because they had not obeyed my laws. (Ezekiel 20 v 23-4)[51]

Looking back many years later, the prophet Zechariah can say God was the primary agent who caused this scattering:

"When I called, they did not listen; so when they called, I would not listen," says the LORD Almighty. "I *scattered* them with a whirlwind among all the nations, where they were strangers." (Zechariah 7:13-14)

Again and again the prophets and the psalms said God would do it: and when it had happened, they said God had done it.

Apart from loyal fellowship with God, human community will always be unstable and the "Tower of Babel" principle will come into play, bringing scattering. This is precisely what happened to the Old Testament people of God.

## The Significance of Babylon

What does Babylon mean in the Bible? In terms of our scattering/gathering tour, I want to focus on three characteristics of Babylon.

### A. Babylon is the opposite of Jerusalem

The most obvious thing about Babylon is it was not Jerusalem. Everything Jerusalem symbolised, Babylon was not. Perhaps the most famous psalm lamenting the exile is Psalm 137. This is a psalm about two cities: Babylon experienced and Zion remembered. Jerusalem is remembered, but the tragedy is it cannot be experienced, and therefore its songs cannot be sung.

> By the rivers of Babylon we sat and wept
>     when we remembered Zion.
> There on the poplars
>     we hung our harps,
> for there our captors asked us for songs,
>     our tormentors demanded songs of joy;
>     they said, "Sing us one of the songs of Zion!"
> How can we sing the songs of the LORD
>     while in a foreign land?
> If I forget you, Jerusalem,
>     may my right hand forget its skill.
> May my tongue cling to the roof of my mouth
>     if I do not remember you,
> if I do not consider Jerusalem
>     my highest joy. (Psalm 137 v 1-6)

The last part of the psalm (v 7-9) expresses in anguished terms the pain of the exiles at being torn away from Jerusalem. The believers amongst them treasured Jerusalem as the place where the people of God gathered in harmony and security in the presence of God under the government of God's Christ.[52] Babylon was the opposite of all of these, a place of scattering rather than harmony, danger rather than security, separation from God and the absence of God's Christ. It is defined by what it is not: there is no vision informing Babylon, no reality, no substance, no life.

## B. Babylon is the place of human pride
Isaiah 13 v 1 – 14 v 23 contains a sustained judgment on Babylon. It emphasises especially the sheer selfish pride of the place. It seems to symbolise the proud sin of the world in general.

> I will punish the world for its evil,
> > the wicked for their sins.
> I will put an end to the arrogance of the haughty
> > and will humble the pride of the ruthless. (13 v 11)

Because it is so proud of its power and achievements, it rides roughshod over others and is a place of oppression and aggression (14 v 4-6). In a strong echo of the builders of the Tower of Babel (Genesis 11 v 4), God says:

> You said in your heart,
> > "I will ascend to the heavens;
> I will raise my throne
> > above the stars of God;
> I will sit enthroned on the mount of assembly,
> > on the utmost heights of Mount Zaphon [i.e. the
> > mountain of God]. (14 v 13)

In Isaiah 47, Babylon expresses her proud heart when she says, "I am, and there is none besides me" (v 8); *I exist for me, and no one else exists except insofar as they do things for me. No one else matters.* The pride of Babylon makes it a selfish place, and therefore a divided place, a place where people treat other people brutally. This was the agonising memory of Psalm 137 v 8-9, remembering the heart-rending cruelty of the Babylonians. Babylon is the very opposite of the city of peace.

## C. Babylon is like hell on earth

Geographically, Babylon may be a location. But relationally, it is a scattering. There may be physical proximity to people, but there is also relational alienation. It is a place where deeply scattered people happen to be living close together. The poet Shelley said that, "Hell is a city much like London": the same could be said of anywhere where community is based on the pride and principles of Babylon. There will be proximity without intimacy, crowdedness without relationship and locality without community.

A terrible and vivid appropriation of the hellish metaphor of Babylon is Kenneth Anger's cult book *Hollywood Babylon*.[53] Anger tells how the "Star system" was born in the 1910s, but how in the midst of the drug-induced euphoria and sexual chaos there was an ever-present fear, "that the bottom could drop out of their gilded dreams at any time". He called Hollywood "the Wonder World of Make Believe", a dream factory (p 7, 15, 17). But it was all so ephemeral and it destroyed so many lives, as Anger catalogues with horrifying detail. Hollywood, like Babylon, was a place of lies, promising pleasure and providing misery.

A friend of mine tells of a bumper sticker that read, "Paratroopers don't die; they just regroup in hell". But they don't: no one "regroups" in hell. Hell is a place of separation, a far cry from the popular idea of a raucous and pleasure-filled party.

C.S. Lewis conveys the sheer loneliness of scattering, in his imaginative novel about Hell, *The Great Divorce*. His narrator is given a bus tour of a vast grey town which seems to go on and on forever but to have hardly anyone living in it. He asks his neighbour on the bus why this is:

> The trouble is that they're so quarrelsome. As soon as anyone arrives he settles in some street. Before he's been there twenty-four hours he quarrels with his neighbour. Before the week is over he's quarrelled so badly that he decides to move. Very likely he finds the next street empty because all the people there have quarrelled with *their* neighbours—and moved. If so he settles in. If by any chance the street is full, he goes further. But even if he stays, it makes no odds. He's sure to have another quarrel pretty soon, and then he'll move on again.[54]

Although Babylon promises all the fun of a raucous pub or a wild orgiastic party, it ends up with a desperate scattered loneliness. In the lonely terrors of hell there is no gathering, no friendship, no love, no loyalty and no affection, nothing to soften the sheer misery of having nothing and no one beyond my selfish self to relate to. This is what Babylon means.

## After Babylon

In the five or so centuries after Babylon, the people of God had to live with two realities in tension. On the one hand, there was a partial and, to be honest, very disappointing "end" to the exile; and yet on the other they carried with them a growing chorus of prophetic voices which insisted God had not given up on his promise to remake the world through Abraham's descendant. Let us consider these in turn.

## A. A partial regathering after the exile

In about 539 BC Cyrus absorbed the neo-Babylonian empire into what later became the vast Persian empire. His policy was to send subject peoples back to their homelands and indeed to encourage them to build temples and worship the gods and goddesses of those lands. The Jews were included in this policy (2 Chronicles 36 v 22-23) and, under the leadership of the scribe Ezra and the political governor Nehemiah, and inspired by the vigorous prophetic preaching of Haggai and Zechariah, several groups of them returned to Jerusalem to rebuild the Temple and the city walls, and to begin again the life of the people of God in what became the province of Judah in the Persian Empire.

Nehemiah sees this political development as the fulfilment of God's promise to gather his scattered people. Before he returns to Jerusalem from the Persian capital Susa, Nehemiah prays and reminds the LORD of his promise:

Remember the instruction you gave your servant Moses, saying, "If you are unfaithful, I will *scatter* you among the nations, but if you return to me and obey my commands, then even if your exiled people are at the farthest horizon, I will *gather* them from there and bring them to the place I have chosen as a dwelling for my Name." (Nehemiah 1 v 8-9)

This programme of resettlement and rebuilding had its setbacks and its encouragements over a number of years, and amongst the encouragements were some very positive gatherings or assemblies.[55] There was one particularly wonderful assembly which must have reminded those with good biblical memories of the foundational assembly at Sinai and the joyful assemblies in Jerusalem before the exile. It is recorded in Nehemiah 8.

> When the seventh month came and the Israelites had settled in their towns, all the people came together as one in the square before the Water Gate. They told Ezra the teacher of the Law to bring out the Book of the Law of Moses, which the Lord had commanded for Israel.
>
> So on the first day of the seventh month Ezra the priest brought the Law before the assembly, which was made up of men and women and all who were able to understand. He read it aloud from daybreak till noon as he faced the square before the Water Gate in the presence of the men, women and others who could understand. And all the people listened attentively to the Book of the Law.
>
> Ezra the teacher of the Law stood on a high wooden platform built for the occasion. Beside him on his right stood Mattithiah, Shema, Anaiah, Uriah, Hilkiah and Maaseiah; and on his left were Pedaiah, Mishael, Malkijah, Hashum, Hashbaddanah, Zechariah and Meshullam.
>
> Ezra opened the book. All the people could see him because he was standing above them; and as he opened it, the people all stood up. Ezra praised the Lord, the great God; and all the people lifted their hands and responded, "Amen! Amen!" Then they bowed down and worshipped the Lord with their faces to the ground.

> The Levites—Jeshua, Bani, Sherebiah, Jamin, Akkub, Shabbethai, Hodiah, Maaseiah, Kelita, Azariah, Jozabad, Hanan and Pelaiah—instructed the people in the Law while the people were standing there. They read from the Book of the Law of God, making it clear and giving the meaning so that the people understood what was being read. (Nehemiah 7 v 73 – 8 v 8)

They assemble as all Israel to hear and obey the word of God. It must have been a wonderful encouragement to taste this joyful assembling of the people of God in Jerusalem again, as the people of God gather in harmony "together as one" (v 1) under the word of God, the pattern of Sinai being worked out again in the life of Israel.

But was the exile really over? If we remember how Psalm 122 celebrated the house of the LORD, the security of the city, the unity of the tribes and the just rule of the king in David's line (see p 99), then we may see there was a very partial re-establishment of the first two but nothing at all to bring back the third and fourth. There was a new Temple, although a very much smaller and poorer one than Solomon's wonderful building. The prophet Haggai asks the Second Temple builders, "Who of you is left who saw this house in its former glory [i.e. Solomon's Temple]? How does it look to you now? Does it not seem to you like nothing?" (Haggai 2 v 3). The city walls were rebuilt which must have just begun to give a fragile sense of security. But the unity of the tribes was never re-established, since the ten "lost tribes" from the former northern kingdom never came back, and indeed the majority of the southern tribes never chose to return from exile. Later, in the time of Esther, the Jews were described as "a certain people *scattered abroad and dispersed* among the peoples in all the provinces" of the Persian empire (Esther 3 v 8 ESV). They formed a great Diaspora (which means "Dispersion" or "Scattering") to the east, south, west and north of the Promised Land. Every time these Diaspora Jews sang Psalm 106 they cried to the LORD:

Save us, LORD our God,
and *gather* us from the nations,
that we may give thanks to your holy name
and glory in your praise. (v 47)

Above all, there was no king, even though Zerubbabel was a descendant of David and some must have hoped he might become king. However, he remained a "governor of Judah", firmly under the thumb of the Persian empire (Haggai 1 v 1; Matthew 1 v 12).

*B. A chorus of prophecies of a reassembled world*
So the promises of a gathered people in fellowship with God, ruled by God's king, and through whom a broken world would be regathered, remained very sadly unfulfilled. And yet—paradoxically—alongside the sad reality of continued scattering, there remained a chorus of voices from all periods of Israel's history, crying out God was going to gather them together at last under Abraham's descendant. Here is a sample of these voices, to help us appreciate just how often the promises for the future were expressed in terms of the gathering of a scattered people. There are more examples that could be chosen.

From the prophet Isaiah:

He will ... *gather* the exiles of Israel; he will *assemble* the scattered people of Judah. (11 v 12)

You, Israel, will be *gathered* up one by one. (27 v 12)

He tends his flock like a shepherd: he *gathers* the lambs in his arms. (40 v 11; notice the link between gathering and shepherding)

I will bring your children from the east and *gather* you from the west. (43 v 5)

… to bring Jacob back to him and *gather* Israel to himself (49 v 5; notice the link between gathering to God and gathering back to one another)

He who *gathers* the exiles of Israel [declares]: "I will *gather* still others to them, besides those already *gathered.*" (56 v 8)

All *assemble* and come to you; your sons come from afar, and your daughters are carried on the hip. (60 v 4)

I … am about to come and *gather* the people of all nations and languages, and they will come and see my glory. (66 v 18)

From the prophet Jeremiah:

I myself will *gather* the remnant of my flock. (23 v 3)

I will *gather* you from all the nations. (29 v 14)

I will … *gather* them from the ends of the earth. (31 v 8)

He who *scattered* Israel will *gather* them and will watch over his flock like a shepherd. (31 v 10)

I will surely *gather* them from all the lands. (32 v 37)

From the prophet Ezekiel:

> Although I sent them far away among the nations and *scattered* them among the countries, yet ... I will *gather* you from the nations and bring you back from the countries where you have been *scattered*. (11 v 16-17)

> When I *gather* the people of Israel from the nations where they have been *scattered*... (28 v 25)

> As a shepherd looks after his *scattered* flock when he is with them, so will I look after my sheep. I will rescue them from all the places where they were *scattered* on a day of clouds and darkness. I will bring them out from the nations and *gather* them from the countries. (34 v 12-13)

> I *dispersed* them among the nations, and they were *scattered* through the countries ... I will *gather* you from all the countries and bring you back into your own land. (36 v 19, 24)

> I will take the Israelites out of the nations where they have gone. I will *gather* them from all around and bring them back into their own land ... There will be *one king* over all of them and they will *never again be two nations or be divided into two kingdoms*. (37 v 21-22)

> When I have brought them back from the nations ... though I sent them into exile ... I will *gather* them. (39 v 27-28)

From the prophet Hosea:

> Yet the Israelites will be like the sand on the seashore, which cannot be measured or counted [echoing the

promise to Abraham]. In the place where it was said to them, "You are not my people", they will be called "children of the living God". The people of Judah and the people of Israel will *come together* [reversing the tearing apart of the kingdom]; they will appoint *one leader* and will come up out of the land [that is, the land of exile]. (1 v 10-11; see also 2 v 14-23)

From the prophet Micah:

I will surely *gather* all of you, Jacob; I will surely *bring together* the remnant of Israel. I will *bring them together* like sheep in a sheepfold, like a flock in its pasture. (2 v 12)

"In that day," declares the LORD, "I will *gather* the lame; I will *assemble* the exiles and those I have brought to grief." (4 v 6)

From the prophet Zephaniah:

From beyond the rivers of Cush my worshippers, my *scattered* people, will bring me offerings … At that time I will deal with all who oppressed you. I will rescue the lame; I will *gather* the exiles. I will give them praise and honour in every land where they have suffered shame. At that time I will *gather* you; at that time I will bring you home. (3 v 10, 19-20)

From the prophet Zechariah:

I will signal for them and *gather* them in. Surely I will redeem them; they will be as numerous as before. Though I *scatter* them among the peoples, yet in distant lands they will remember me. (10 v 8-9)

All these prophecies insist that God is going to do a great gathering, even though it was painfully obvious that, even by the very end of the Old Testament period, he had not done it yet.

## Conclusion

Again and again, these voices from God reaffirmed the promise to Abraham, that in his descendant the whole world would be blessed and there would be a great gathering. The scattering of Israel's Old Testament history would one day be reversed. What do we learn from putting these voices alongside the Old Testament realities of Israel's life? The reality was that Israel was, for the most part, indistinguishable from the rest of the world east of Eden, scattered from the Tower of Babel. Their wonderful history ended, more or less, in Babylon, right back at Babel again.

We learn from this that the assemblies patterned for us at Sinai and then Jerusalem were foreshadowings of the gatherings God would do to fulfil his promise to Abraham, but were not the gatherings themselves. They were realistic practice exercises to show us what the real gatherings would be like. These assemblies were, as it were, scale models of the real thing. Although all through Israel's history there were some real believers, by and large Old Testament Israel did not exhibit the evidence of being the true people of God. So these assemblies are in the Bible to show us the pattern for the real gatherings, which are the assemblies of the local Christian church. These churches, the realisation (that is to say, the "making real") of the promise of God, did not become possible until two great New Testament events had taken place: the Cross of Christ and the outpouring of the Holy Spirit at Pentecost. These great events are the subjects for the next two chapters.

## Questions for Discussion

1. Review the survey in this chapter of what happened from Jerusalem to Babylon. What were the main stages in the disintegration of the people of God? What caused this?

2. Have you seen the pride of Babylon in our society, in leaders and in your own heart? How does it express itself?

3. Have you experienced "places" like Babylon—places of relational scattering in which people are alienated from one another?

4. How do these experiences serve to warn us of the lonely terrors of hell?

5. Review what happened after the exile in Babylon. In what ways was it disappointing, and in what ways encouraging?

6. How can the life of a local church answer in practice the longings of lonely people?

ALL HUMANITY

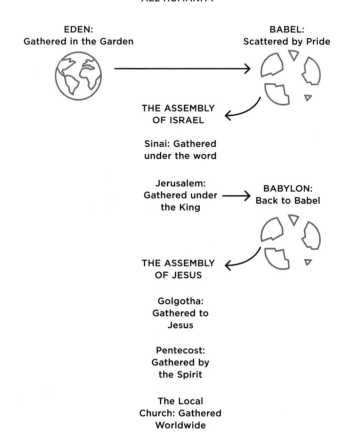

EDEN:
Gathered in the Garden

BABEL:
Scattered by Pride

THE ASSEMBLY
OF ISRAEL

Sinai: Gathered
under the word

Jerusalem:
Gathered under
the King

BABYLON:
Back to Babel

THE ASSEMBLY
OF JESUS

Golgotha:
Gathered to
Jesus

Pentecost:
Gathered by
the Spirit

The Local
Church: Gathered
Worldwide

# The Assembly of Jesus: Gathering Realised

# SIX

# Golgotha: Gathered to Jesus

O ur Bible tour takes us now to the centre of human history and the place where all the gatherings and scatterings of the Old Testament begin to make sense, "Golgotha ... 'the place of the skull'" where they crucified Jesus (Mark 15 v 22). The Bible story so far is full of puzzles. One big puzzle is this: on the one hand we have a broken world, excluded from Eden, shattered and living in the long shadow of the Tower of Babel. This is the consequence of human pride and rebellion against God. On the other hand, we have the promise of God who has said he will reunite the world through Abraham's descendant, and seemed to begin to do that through the assembly at Sinai and then the joyful gatherings at Zion. And yet now our story is (spiritually) scattered in Babylon; we might as well be back at the Tower of Babel. So how is the God who promised to reunite the world going to keep his promise?

## The Earthly Ministry of Jesus
*Expectations of gathering*
What would a believing Jew have been thinking around the year zero, between what we now call BC and AD? We meet one

such believer in Luke 2 v 25-35. His name is Simeon and he is one of my favourite minor characters in the Bible; I think he should be nominated for a Bible Oscar for "Best Supporting Actor". When Simeon is introduced, Jesus was very young, and Joseph and Mary were taking him to the Temple for a Jewish ceremony.

Luke introduces him like this: "Now there was a man in Jerusalem called Simeon, who was righteous and devout" (v 25). This didn't just mean he kept the Law of Moses outwardly: it also meant that in his heart he loved God and believed the promises God had made to Abraham. Because he believed the promises, Luke goes on, "He was waiting for the consolation of Israel". Simeon would have been painfully aware of living in a broken world, and could no doubt have sung Psalm 120 with feeling (see p 89). He knew God had promised to remake the broken world through Abraham's descendant. He remembered the amazing assembly at Mount Sinai (how could any pious Jew forget!) and he treasured all Jerusalem symbolised in the promises of God. But he knew it had all ended in tears and scattering, finally to Babylon. And in his heart he seems to have known this scattering had never really ended. There was still no sign of an assembly of nations, the real United Nations, through Abraham's descendant (Genesis 28 v 3; 35 v 11; 48 v 4). Most deeply, he felt the pain of Israel that there was not yet the promised king in David's line, the Messiah or Christ. How could the world be remade until God's Christ came? Only this descendant of Abraham could be "the consolation of Israel", the one who fulfils the promises to Abraham, and remakes a broken world.

Wonderfully, God had revealed to Simeon that he would not die before he had seen God's Messiah. It must have been very surprising for Joseph and Mary as they took the baby Jesus into the Temple and were met by this man, who took the baby in his arms and began to pray:

> Sovereign Lord, as you have promised,
>> you may now dismiss your servant in peace.
> For my eyes have seen your salvation,
>> which you have prepared in the sight of all nations,
> a light for revelation to the Gentiles,
>> and the glory of your people Israel. (Luke 2 v 29-32)

Simeon understood this child was God's Christ who would bring a rescue to finally remake a broken world. Mary herself had sung a Spirit-inspired song during her pregnancy, in which she had celebrated that God...

> ...has scattered those who are proud in their inmost thoughts ...
>> but has lifted up the humble ...
> He has helped his servant Israel,
>> remembering to be merciful
> to Abraham and his descendants for ever,
>> just as he promised our ancestors. (Luke 1 v 51-55)

Mary knew about the scattering of Babel, the scattering of the proud, and she had just begun to understand that her baby would be the one through whom God kept his promises to Abraham. So maybe when she thought about it, Simeon's song won't have come as such a surprise.

Matthew too drops a big hint that Jesus came to gather. He begins his Gospel with a carefully structured genealogy of Jesus.

> This is the genealogy of *Jesus the Messiah* the son of *David*, the son of *Abraham*:

*Abraham* was the father of [thirteen generations before] King *David*,

*David* was the father of [thirteen generations before] Josiah the father of Jeconiah and his brothers at the time of *the exile to Babylon.*

After *the exile to Babylon*: [there were thirteen generations before] Joseph, the husband of Mary, and Mary was the mother of *Jesus who is called the Messiah.*

Thus there were fourteen generations in all from *Abraham* to *David*, fourteen from *David* to *the exile to Babylon*, and fourteen from *the exile* to *the Messiah.*

(Matthew 1 v 1-17)

By artificially missing out some of the generations, Matthew structures his genealogy to make the point that there are three critical people or events to bear in mind when thinking about the Christ (Messiah). These are (a) Abraham (who was promised his offspring would inherit the world), (b) David (who was promised he would rule the world from Zion), and (c) the exile to Babylon. So Jesus Christ will be: (a) "the son of Abraham", i.e. the descendant of Abraham who will inherit the world; (b) "the son of David" who will rule the world in justice from "Zion"; and (c) at last the one who brings the scattering of exile to an end. Jesus is the Christ who will gather a broken world together again under the rule of the one God.

The apostle Paul wrote that "no matter how many promises God has made, they are 'Yes' in Christ" (2 Corinthians 1 v 20). Given that so many of these promises are couched in the language of a great gathering, we shall not be surprised to find Jesus Christ is the key to this gathering.

*The earthly ministry of Jesus who gathers his church*

When Jesus of Nazareth was about thirty years old, a massive religious movement swept Judea. At the centre of it was a strange man called John the Baptist, a powerful preacher of repentance. John made it clear his was just a preparatory movement to get ready for Jesus, who was much greater than himself. One of the ways he described this much greater man was in terms of a farmer at harvest:

> His winnowing fork is in his hand, and he will clear his threshing-floor, *gathering* his wheat into the barn and burning up the chaff with unquenchable fire.
>
> (Matthew 3 v 12)

Gathering is what Jesus does. From the moment he started his public ministry, Jesus began to gather. Right at the start he called disciples to follow him, and said they too would become gatherers, fishers of people.

> As Jesus was walking beside the Sea of Galilee, he saw two brothers, Simon called Peter and his brother Andrew. They were casting a net into the lake, for they were fishermen. "Come, follow me," Jesus said, "and *I will send you out to fish for people.*" At once they left their nets and followed him.
>
> Going on from there, he saw two other brothers, James son of Zebedee and his brother John. They were in a boat with their father Zebedee, preparing their nets. Jesus called them, and immediately they left the boat and their father and followed him.
>
> (Matthew 4 v 18-22)

Jesus gathers; and those he gathers begin to gather with him.

Crowds flocked to him (see, for example, Matthew 4 v 23 – 5 v 1). Jesus was a magnet. He reached out especially to outsiders and unlikely people. To the leper, by definition excluded both from God's presence in the Temple and from the people of God, Jesus reached out his hand: he touched him, made him well and brought him in (Matthew 8 v 1-4). He ate in fellowship with the despised tax-collectors and notorious "sinners", calling one of them to be an apostle; he was known as the friend of sinners (Matthew 9 v 9-11; 11 v 19). It was a characteristic mark of his ministry that "tax collectors and sinners were all gathering round to hear him" (Luke 15 v 1). He declares that one chief tax-collector is "a son of Abraham", bringing him in to Abraham's people (Luke 19 v 9). We saw in Chapter 1 that death is the cruellest and most painful form of separation or scattering. So it is not surprising to find in Jesus' earthly ministry that he gathers people from death itself. He meets a mother grieving her dead son who has been separated from her by death, restores the young man to life and gives him back to his mother; mother and son become, as we might say, a reassembled family (Luke 7 v 11-17)!

In an echo of Old Testament shepherd passages (especially Ezekiel 34), Jesus looks at the crowds and longs to gather them in, as a farmer gathers a harvest into a barn or a shepherd his sheep into a sheepfold.

Jesus went through all the towns and villages, teaching in their synagogues, proclaiming the good news of the kingdom and healing every disease and illness. When he saw the crowds, he had compassion on them, because they were harassed and helpless, like sheep without a shepherd. Then he said to his disciples, "The harvest is plentiful but the workers are few. Ask the Lord of the harvest, therefore, to send out workers into his harvest field." (Matthew 9 v 35-38)

He tells his disciples he is determined to build his "church", his assembly (Matthew 16 v 18). The Old Testament Assembly of Israel pointed forward to the Assembly of Jesus. One day he will return to this earth to "gather his elect from the four winds, from one end of the heavens to the other" (Matthew 24 v 31).

In an important "gathering" section of John's Gospel (John 9 and 10), Jesus first reaches an outsider, a man born blind, a man who most people thought was tainted in some dangerous way by sin (9 v 1-2). Jesus brings this man in, and is vigorously opposed by the Pharisees, who would have been happy to keep him outside. Jesus follows up this controversy by speaking of himself as the Good Shepherd, again picking up Old Testament "shepherd" passages. Jesus is the only truly good leader for the people of God: and he is also the one who will at last gather them from all over the world.

> I am the good shepherd; I know my sheep and my sheep know me—just as the Father knows me and I know the Father—and I lay down my life for the sheep. I have other sheep that are not of this sheepfold. I must bring them also. They too will listen to my voice, and there shall be *one flock and one shepherd*. (John 10 v 14-16)

It is vital to Jesus' ministry both that he gathers, and that those he gathers become gatherers of all sorts of other people. Indeed, "whoever who does not gather with me scatters" (Matthew 12 v 30). There is no neutral position: Jesus is like a magnet who magnetizes the iron filings attracted to himself. Gathering is vital and central to what Jesus does.

*And yet Jesus also divides*

And yet, although gathering is what Jesus does and is the activity close to his heart, he warns that his gathering will also divide, because not all will submit to be gathered to him.

Do not suppose that I have come to bring peace to the earth. I did not come to bring peace, but a sword. For I have come to turn

"a man against his father,
    a daughter against her mother,
a daughter-in-law against her mother-in-law—
    a man's enemies will be the members of his own
    household."

Anyone who loves their father or mother more than me is not worthy of me; anyone who loves their son or daughter more than me is not worthy of me. Whoever does not take up their cross and follow me is not worthy of me. Whoever finds their life will lose it, and whoever loses their life for my sake will find it.
(Matthew 10 v 34-39; see also Luke 12 v 49-53)

In the parable of the wedding banquet Jesus speaks of the kingdom of heaven as a feast from which those first invited excuse themselves, but at which all sorts of unlikely people find themselves gathered and seated in the end (Matthew 22 v 1-14; Luke 14 v 15-24).

Shortly before the end of his earthly life, he laments the refusal of so many in Jerusalem to let him gather them in.

Jerusalem, Jerusalem, you who kill the prophets and stone those sent to you, how often I have longed to gather your children together, as a hen gathers her chicks under her wings, and you were not willing.

(Matthew 23 v 37)

The only people who were excluded from his welcome were those who were sure they didn't need it and despised those who knew they did need it.

> As Jesus went on from there, he saw a man named Matthew sitting at the tax collector's booth. "Follow me," he told him, and Matthew got up and followed him.

> While Jesus was having dinner at Matthew's house, many tax collectors and sinners came and ate with him and his disciples. When the Pharisees saw this, they asked his disciples, "Why does your teacher eat with tax collectors and sinners?"

> On hearing this, Jesus said, "It is not the healthy who need a doctor, but those who are ill. But go and learn what this means: "I desire mercy, not sacrifice." For I have not come to call the righteous, but sinners."

> (Matthew 9 v 9-13)

Jesus gathers: but some will be left outside. He gathers all kinds of people without distinction of race, culture, class, or moral respectability. But he does not gather all people without exception. Some despise his gathering grace. He came as a doctor for the sick; the only people excluded from his welcome are those who insist they are not sick (and thereby show they are deluded).

Commending the faith of a Gentile Roman centurion, he said that in the great gathering at the end of time there would be some surprising people included (those who trusted him) and some horrified people excluded (horrified, because they thought they deserved to be insiders). There will be a terrible "outside", a place of eternal exile, a scattering with no return.

> I say to you that many will come from the east and the
> west, and will take their places at the feast with
> Abraham, Isaac and Jacob in the kingdom of heaven.
> But the subjects of the kingdom will be thrown outside,
> into the darkness, where there will be weeping and
> gnashing of teeth. (Matthew 8 v 11-12)

So the earthly ministry of Jesus shows us both gathering and exclusion. All sorts of unlikely men and women are gathered into Jesus' church, his assembly; and yet all sorts of surprised people, who thought they ought to be insiders, find themselves outside of Jesus' church. We shall understand this only at the Cross, because it is only by the scandalous death of Jesus that he can gather his church, and it is those who are offended by the Cross who exclude themselves from his church.

## Gathered at Golgotha: Only at the Cross of Jesus is a Broken World Remade

During Jesus' earthly ministry his apostles saw all sorts of things they did not fully understand at the time. When the Gospels were written later, they sometimes put in explanatory comments to show what the events and teaching of Jesus' life meant. Matthew includes one of these comments in the middle of an account of Jesus' healing ministry.

> When evening came, many who were demon-possessed
> were brought to [Jesus], and he drove out the spirits with
> a word and healed all who were ill. This was to fulfil
> what was spoken through the prophet Isaiah:

"He took up our infirmities
and bore our diseases." (Matthew 8 v 16-17)

Matthew quotes from one of the famous songs in Isaiah about a future "Servant of the Lord", which means someone who is in faithful covenant relationship with the Lord. The song Matthew quotes from is Isaiah 52 v 13 – 53 v 12 and includes the prophecy that this Servant will suffer and die to pay the penalty for the sins of the people. I doubt if Matthew understood this at the time, but later when he wrote his Gospel he saw that Jesus could only heal and gather during his earthly ministry because he was going to die to pay the penalty for sinners.

As Jesus' earthly ministry continued, those with him saw all manner of wonderful examples of gathering as Jesus healed, forgave, and brought men and women into his new community, his church. But as time drew on there was a mounting sense of foreboding: for Jesus said again and again he was going to be killed (Mark 8 v 31; 9 v 31; 10 v 33-34).

When the Jewish leaders were plotting to kill Jesus, Caiaphas the high priest said something more profound than he realised:

Then one of them, named Caiaphas, who was high
priest that year, spoke up, "You know nothing at all!
You do not realise that it is better for you that one man
die for the people than that the whole nation perish."
(John 11 v 49-50)

What Caiaphas meant was a simple truth of realpolitik: it would be better for this tiresome imposter and troublemaker to be killed, than to allow him to start a rebellion the Romans would surely crush and so destroy the whole nation. But John goes on to explain there was something deeper going on than even Caiaphas the speaker realised:

> He did not say this on his own, but as high priest that
> year he prophesied that Jesus would die for the Jewish
> nation, and not only for that nation but also for the
> scattered children of God, to bring them together and
> make them one. (John 11 v 51-52)

Caiaphas spoke more truly than he realised: he prophesied, that is, he said what God wanted said. The full God-given meaning of what he said is an extraordinarily vivid echo of our theme of scattering and gathering. Jesus will die in order "to bring together" "the scattered children of God" "and make them one": that is, he will die finally to bring to an end all that the exile symbolised, that terrible scattering we saw at the Tower of Babel, and the exclusion from the garden of Eden. All the scattering of a broken world will be healed and gathered at the Cross of Jesus Christ.

Jesus himself understood this. As he anticipates the Cross, he says, "I, when I am lifted up from the earth" (that is, lifted up on the cross) "will draw all people" (that is, all kinds of people without distinction) "to myself" (John 12 v 32). Jesus does not promise to draw or gather all human beings without exception to himself. Elsewhere he has made it clear some will be excluded (e.g. Matthew 8 v 10-12). He means that on the cross he will draw to himself all kinds of people without distinction of race, gender, moral respectability, privilege, culture or talents. In particular, he will gather to himself, into his church, people who failed to fulfil the Law of Moses.

The Law of Moses was the great divider of humanity in the culture and land of Jesus: either you were in or you were out. The great guardians of the law were the Pharisees, who were quite sure they were in and most other people were out. The surprise was that the people who thought they were in were actually out, and all sorts of people who were regarded as being out were drawn in by Jesus. Jesus was very rude about the people who were sure they were "righteous" and called them "white-washed tombs", with the outward appearance of being clean but actually being very dirty inside (Matthew 23 v 27-28). These are the people who think of themselves as being members of the kingdom of God, but who will end up "thrown outside, into the darkness, where there will be weeping and gnashing of teeth" (Matthew 8 v 12). This must prompt us to ask how anyone can get inside, be gathered into the people of God.

We need to think back in our Bible journey to the covenant curses of scattering. We saw at the Tower of Babel that God scatters the proud. He always has, he always does, and he always will. When he made a covenant with his people, he called them to depend on him in humble trust, to believe his promises to Abraham and to live as faithful and obedient people. If they don't, then again and again God warns them they will be scattered: this is exactly what happened (see p 107-110). The law of God given at Sinai is a very good law. If people lived like that then humanity would be wonderfully united and harmonious-ly gathered. There would be no need for policemen, for locks, for aid agencies; there would be no hunger, no poverty, no war and no cruelty. But we don't and we won't live like this because our hearts are the same as the hearts of the builders of the Tower of Babel. We live under the curse of the law, and it is entirely our fault.

What happened at the Cross of Jesus is that God took upon himself in the person of his Son the curse of the law. There is an Old Testament law that says a person who is "hung on a pole" (public execution and disgrace) is "under God's curse" (Deuteronomy 21 v 22-23). Their public execution is a sign that they are guilty and rightly condemned by God. When

Jesus died on a wooden cross, the early Christians understood that his public disgrace meant exactly this: he was under the curse of God. So Paul writes:

Christ redeemed us from the curse of the law by becoming a curse for us, for it is written: "Cursed is everyone who is hung on a pole." (Galatians 3 v 13)

God made him who had no sin to be sin for us.
(2 Corinthians 5 v 21)

All the right and fair hot anger of God against sinners was poured out on God at the Cross of Jesus. He became "sin"; he became "a curse"; and he did it "for us". Books have been written, will be written, and ought to go on being written, on the wonderful truth of the Cross.[56] But for the purposes of our thematic study, I want us to notice only this sin-bearing death, this death that takes on itself the wrath of God, is able to reconcile human beings to God—and therefore make it possible for human beings to be reconciled to one another.

The reason the Cross is the focus of worldwide gathering is that only at the Cross does God make peace between God and sinful people. Only at the Cross are we given peace and reconciliation with God (Romans 5 v 1, 10-11). And therefore only at the Cross can we be reconciled to our fellow human beings.

Jesus came as the doctor to those who know they need healing. Those who are happy as they are, confident in their own ability to live in proud autonomy, exclude themselves from his healing and gathering work. The Cross is both the focus of worldwide gathering and at the same time the great divider. It is offensive to human pride to be told I can contribute nothing to my right standing with God, and to be told I cannot build stable lasting human society without Jesus dying to pay the penalty for my sin. I would much prefer to think I can do it on my own. Only those who are humbled by the Cross can live together in love and harmony, because only those men and women have nothing to prove and nothing to hide. In Chapter 8 we shall explore much more fully what the Cross means for the local church, and how the local church can only experience real God-given unity at the foot of the Cross.

The President of the United States is sometimes called "the leader of the free world". It is a fine title and there have been times when the world has had cause to be very grateful to America and some American presidents. But ultimately there is only one man who is qualified to bear this title. He bears it because he alone has done what was necessary to bring a broken and enslaved world into freedom, peace and unity. It is because the Cross is so utterly crucial (literally) to the remaking of a broken world that only Jesus can be the leader of that new world. One day the world will bow the knee to the one who died. This is why he alone can be entrusted with "all authority in heaven and on earth" (Matthew 28 v 18). This is why Paul can call people from all over the world to bow the knee in "the obedience that comes from faith" in Jesus (Philippians 2 v 6-11; Romans 1 v 5, 16 v 26).

## Questions for Discussion

1. Review what we have seen of the earthly ministry of Jesus. How have we seen him acting as a magnet to draw people together? Can you think of other examples from the Gospels?

2. What kinds of people kept their distance from Jesus, and why?

3. Why is the Cross the only way to draw all kinds of people together?

4. Why do some people find this offensive?

5. Have you seen the local church becoming a magnet for all kinds of needy people, as Jesus was?

6. If not, what is stopping this happening? How can we help outsiders understand that we are not superior to them, but invite them to join us at the foot of the Cross?

# SEVEN

# Pentecost: Gathered by the Spirit

In our tour of the Bible, we have made some long journeys between our main stops. From Sinai to Jerusalem took hundreds of years: so did Jerusalem to Babylon, and Babylon to Golgotha. Our next journey takes just a few weeks: but what amazing weeks! We move now from that earth-changing day at the Cross to a day just a few weeks later, also in Jerusalem, at the Jewish festival of Pentecost. Before we get there, however, we need to wind back the clock to some prophecies given in exile in Babylon.

## The Promise of the Spirit to Gather the People of God

We have seen Israel was given a chorus of prophecies that one day God would remake his broken world (see p 121-125). We are going to focus now on the prophecies in Ezekiel 34–37: we shall see these prophecies connect the gathering of Israel with the outpouring of the Spirit of God.

Ezekiel 34 is a sustained judgment on the selfish and unfaithful leaders (shepherds) of Israel. As a result of their evil leadership God's "sheep" have been "scattered" and "became food for all the wild animals. My sheep wandered over all the mountains and on every high hill. They were scattered over the whole earth, and no one searched or looked for them" (v 5-6). Because the shepherds are not doing their job, God promises he will do it himself: "As a shepherd looks after his scattered flock when he is with them, so will I look after my sheep. I will rescue them from all the places where they were scattered on a day of clouds and darkness. I will bring them out of the nations and gather them from the countries, and I will bring them into their own land" (v 12-13). He will do this by placing over them "one shepherd, my servant David, and he will tend them" (v 23).

Ezekiel 36 v 24-38 comes back to this theme of gathering: "For I will take you out of the nations; I will gather you from all the countries and bring you back into your own land." But this time the focus is on the people themselves, and their need for cleansing and forgiveness: "I will sprinkle clean water on you, and you will be clean; I will cleanse you from all your impurities and from all your idols. I will give you a new heart and put a new spirit in you; I will remove from you your heart of stone and give you a heart of flesh. And I will put my Spirit in you and move you to follow my decrees and be careful to keep my laws" (v 24-27). Only a people whose hearts are changed can live in the land securely and harmoniously gathered, because only this people will live in harmony with God's peace-giving way of life (his law). This change of heart can only come about by a spiritual heart transplant, which is the work of the Spirit of God himself.

This prophecy is immediately followed by the famous prophecy of the valley of dry bones in Ezekiel 37 v 1-14:

The hand of the Lord was on me, and he brought me out by the Spirit of the Lord and set me in the middle of a valley; it was full of bones. He led me to and fro among them, and I saw a great many bones on the floor of the valley, bones that were very dry. He asked me, "Son of man, can these bones live?"

I said, "Sovereign Lord, you alone know."

Then he said to me, "Prophesy to these bones and say to them, 'Dry bones, hear the word of the Lord! This is what the Sovereign Lord says to these bones: I will make breath enter you, and you will come to life. I will attach tendons to you and make flesh come upon you and cover you with skin; I will put breath in you, and you will come to life. Then you will know that I am the Lord.'"

So I prophesied as I was commanded. And as I was prophesying, there was a noise, a rattling sound, and the bones came together, bone to bone. I looked, and tendons and flesh appeared on them and skin covered them, but there was no breath in them.

Then he said to me, "Prophesy to the breath; prophesy, son of man, and say to it, 'This is what the Sovereign Lord says: come, breath, from the four winds and breathe into these slain, that they may live.'" So I prophesied as he commanded me, and breath entered them; they came to life and stood up on their feet—a vast army.

Then he said to me: "Son of man, these bones are the people of Israel. They say, 'Our bones are dried up and our hope is gone; we are cut off.' Therefore prophesy and say to them: 'This is what the Sovereign Lord says: my people, I am going to open your graves and bring you up from them; I will bring you back to the land of Israel. Then you, my people, will know that I am the Lord, when I open your graves and bring you up from them. I will put my Spirit in you and you will live, and I will settle you in your own land. Then you will know that I the Lord have spoken, and I have done it, declares the Lord.'"

The dry bones are a picture of a scattered Israel under judgment. This is clear from verse 11: "these bones are the people of Israel. They say, 'Our bones are dried up and our hope is gone; we are cut off.'" In the vision, Israel is reconnected with itself in every way, gathered together to become "a vast army" whom God will "bring ... back to the land of Israel" (v 10, 12). It is a picture of a supernatural gathering that will follow the scattering of exile. The climax of the vision is in verse 14: "I will put my Spirit in you and you will live". The "breath" Ezekiel breathed in the vision is the same word as "spirit", and pictures the breath or Spirit of God put inside the people of God to change them and give them life on the inside.

Immediately after this, in Ezekiel 37 v 15-28 we have a wonderful prophecy of a reunited north and south in Israel. Ezekiel is to take two sticks of wood and write the name of the southern kingdom on one and the northern kingdom on the other. Then he is to "Join them together into one stick so that they will become one in your hand" (v 15-17). When asked to explain this prophetic visual aid, he is to say, "This is what the Sovereign LORD says: I will take the Israelites out of the nations where they have gone. I will gather them from all around and bring them back into their own land. I will make them one nation in the land, on the mountains of Israel. There will be one king over all of them and they will never again be two nations or be divided into two kingdoms … My servant David will be king over them, and they will all have one shepherd" (v 21-22, 24).

Putting these prophecies together we see that the gathering of Israel, which is itself the beginning of the reversal of the scattering of Babel, will only happen when the Spirit of God is poured into the hearts of the whole people of God. Gathering cannot happen without the Spirit.

### The Spirit and the Cross

The gift of the Spirit to the people of God will usher in the age of reconnection. But why the Cross? Why did Jesus need to die? Why could God not just decide it was time to pour out his Spirit on his people and gather them again? We can begin to understand the reason from John's Gospel. In John 1 v 29-34, John the Baptist first says, "Look, the Lamb of God, who takes away the sin of the world!" and only then says, "The man on whom you see the Spirit come down and remain is the one who will baptise with the Holy Spirit" (v 29, 33). To "baptise with the Holy Spirit" means to pour the Spirit of God into a human being so the person of God himself dwells inside him or her for ever. This is what happens when a man or woman becomes a real Christian. But only Jesus can give this gift. John the Baptist is filled with wonder that Jesus will have the power to pour the very presence and person of God himself into a human heart: he knows no other religious leader, teacher or preacher can do this. He himself can baptise with water, giving the outward sign, but he cannot change a human heart (Matthew 3 v 11). And yet it becomes clear that the only reason Jesus has this power is because he is the Lamb of God who dies on the cross to take away sin.

Although the Spirit of God has been active ever since Creation, he could not be poured into human hearts in this lasting and permanent way until Jesus had died. In John 7, on the last day of the feast of Tabernacles, Jesus speaks about streams of living water flowing and bringing life (v 37-38). John explains, "By this [Jesus] meant the Spirit, whom those who believed in him were later to receive. Up to that time the Spirit had not been given, since Jesus had not yet been glorified"; that is, glorified by being lifted up on the cross (v 39).

The reason the Spirit could not be given until Jesus had died for sinners on the cross is that if God came into an uncleansed human heart, he would destroy us. Because he is the Spirit of God, he is the Spirit of utter all-consuming holiness, the Holy Spirit: and holiness will destroy us unless our sin is cleansed by the Cross. To have the Spirit of the Holy God invading uncleansed human hearts would be like the people of Israel at Sinai wandering onto the mountain: it would have been more than their lives were worth. It is no light thing to have him in our hearts. This is why Jesus had first to die and only then could the Spirit be poured out to live in human hearts for ever.

In the previous chapter we looked at Galatians 3 v 13, where Paul speaks of Jesus "becoming a curse for us" (see p 143-144). In the next verse he tells us why Jesus did this:

> Christ redeemed us from the curse of the law by becoming a curse for us, for it is written: "Cursed is everyone who is hung on a pole." He redeemed us *in order that* the blessing given to Abraham might come to the

Gentiles through Christ Jesus, so that by faith we might receive the promise of the Spirit. (3 v 13-14)

Jesus died so "the blessing given to Abraham" (that is, the gospel promise that his offspring would inherit the world, Romans 4 v 13) might spread right round the world ("come to the Gentiles"), so that anyone who comes to Jesus in faith would "receive the promise of the Spirit". The promise of the Spirit is central to the fulfilment of the promise to Abraham. The promise to Abraham can only be fulfilled when Jesus bears the curse and the Spirit is poured out on all who believe. Only the gift of the Spirit can enable the regathering of a broken world.

## Pentecost: the Reversal of Babel

So after Jesus has died, and been raised from the dead as the proof his death has been effective, we are not surprised that he tells his disciples to wait for the outpouring of the Spirit:

Do not leave Jerusalem, but wait for the gift my Father promised, which you have heard me speak about. For John [the Baptist] baptised with water, but in a few days you will be baptised with the Holy Spirit. (Acts 1 v 4-5)

They waited. While they waited, they appointed Matthias to replace Judas Iscariot and bring the number of the apostles back up to the symbolic number Twelve, a sign they were heads of a reconstituted or regathered Israel (Acts 1 v 12-26). And then:

When the day of Pentecost came, they were all together in one place. Suddenly a sound like the blowing of a violent wind came from heaven and filled the whole house where they were sitting. They saw what seemed to be tongues of fire that separated and came to rest on each of them. All of them were filled with the Holy Spirit and began to speak in other tongues as the Spirit enabled them.

Now there were staying in Jerusalem God-fearing Jews from every nation under heaven. When they heard this sound, a crowd came together in bewilderment, because each one heard their own language being spoken. Utterly amazed, they asked: "Aren't all these who are speaking Galileans? Then how is it that each of us hears them in our native language? Parthians, Medes and Elamites; residents of Mesopotamia, Judea and Cappadocia, Pontus and Asia, Phrygia and Pamphylia, Egypt and the parts of Libya near Cyrene; visitors from Rome (both Jews and converts to Judaism); Cretans and Arabs—we hear them declaring the wonders of God in our own tongues!" Amazed and perplexed, they asked one another, "What does this mean?" (Acts 2 v 1-12)

The believers "were all together in one place" (v 1), as an assembly or gathering. But staying in Jerusalem at the same time were "God-fearing Jews from every nation under heaven" (v 5). Most of those could not have understood the little assembly of disciples if they had tried; they lived in the long shadow of the Tower of Babel. Ever since the Tower of Babel, the confusion of human languages, and the difficulties human beings have communicating properly, have been a terrible sign of living in the world outside Eden, the world under God's righteous curse on human pride.

Now, wonderfully and very surprisingly, the confusion of languages is briefly and miraculously overcome. Babel is reversed. At Babel the people sang their own praises, and so became incomprehensible to one another: at Pentecost, they sang the praises of the one God, and so began to understand one another. It is still now a wonderful thing to hear Christian brothers and sisters sing the praises of God, even when we cannot understand them. I remember on my first Sunday visiting a church in Japan listening as they sang a hymn in Japanese. Unlike the day of Pentecost, I didn't understand a word: but I had tears in my eyes as it came home to me one day we would understand one another perfectly, singing the praises of God and the Lamb for ever around the throne. The first Christian Pentecost anticipated that great day.

When the people ask Peter, "What does this mean?" (v 12), Peter preaches his famous Pentecost sermon, proclaiming to them the death, resurrection, ascension and glorification of Jesus as Lord and Messiah (v 14-36). When they ask, "What shall we do?" (v 37) he says:

> Repent and be baptised, every one of you, in the name of Jesus Christ for the forgiveness of your sins. And you will receive the gift of the Holy Spirit. The promise is for you and your children and for all who are far off—for all whom the Lord our God will call. (Acts 2 v 38-39)

The twin promises of forgiveness and the gift of the Spirit are given not only to Peter's hearers (mainly Jewish with a few proselytes), but also "for all who are far off—for all whom the Lord our God will call". This gospel gift, the Spirit of God given to every forgiven man and woman, will regather the scattered people of God and bring them together as one at last. He will remake a broken world.

This theme of a gathering spreading all over the world develops as the story of Acts is told. For example, in one of Peter's speeches he says his hearers are "heirs of the prophets and of the covenant God made with your fathers. He said to Abraham, 'Through your offspring all peoples on earth will be blessed'" (Acts 3 v 25). The promise spreads to Samaria, that messed-up region that testified to the miserable scattering of the northern kingdom by Assyria in 729 BC (see p 109-110); and then the regathering spreads right out to the Gentiles (from Acts 10 onwards). This is God by his Spirit beginning the work of remaking a broken world.

## The Spirit of Unity

The reason the Spirit brings men and women together is that he is the Spirit of the God who is One (see p 11-12). By bringing men and women into fellowship with God, he brings them into harmony with one another. You and I cannot re-enter Eden without finding ourselves side by side with one another. In London there are some squares surrounded by houses, with a communal garden in the middle, shared by all the residents. Eden is more like this than individual little gardens in which each of us can enjoy fellowship with God on our own! There is one garden, where the God who is One walks with his people.

In 1 Corinthians Paul writes to a church riven with selfish divisions and overexcited about the gifts given by the risen Christ to his people by his Spirit, wanting to use those gifts to puff themselves up. To this divided church Paul writes about the oneness of God:

> There are different kinds of gifts, but the same Spirit distributes them. There are different kinds of service, but the same Lord. There are different kinds of working, but in all of them and in everyone it is the same God at work. (1 Corinthians 12 v 4-6)

Paul's point is there is one true God, Father, Son and Holy Spirit. There are not three gods, but one God in three persons. So when the Spirit of God really works in human hearts, he brings them together. He is "not a God of disorder but of peace" (14 v 33). The only reason Christians can ever manage to get along together in harmony is we have been given the Spirit of the God who is One.

Paul uses similar arguments in Ephesians 4:

Make every effort to keep the unity of the Spirit through the bond of peace. There is one body and one Spirit, just as you were called to one hope when you were called; one Lord, one faith, one baptism; one God and Father of all, who is over all and through all and in all. (v 3-6)

The reason the various gifts are given is...

...so that the body of Christ may be built up until we all reach unity in the faith and in the knowledge of the Son of God and become mature. (v 12-13)

## Gathered into the Fellowship of the Trinity

The deepest sense in which the Spirit of God gathers the people of God is he draws us into the fellowship of the Trinity. In thinking about this we are on holy ground. In the prologue to John's Gospel, John tells us Jesus gives those who receive him the right to become children of God, to be gathered into the family of God:

[the Word] came to that which was his own, but his own did not receive him. Yet to all who did receive him, to those who believed in his name, he gave the right to become children of God—children born not of natural descent, nor of human decision or a husband's will, but born of God. (John 1 v 11-13)

We are gathered into the family of God by a supernatural birth ("born of God"). We begin to understand how this supernatural birth can happen when Jesus speaks with the Jewish leader Nicodemus one night:

Now there was a Pharisee, a man named Nicodemus who was a member of the Jewish ruling council. He came to Jesus at night and said, "Rabbi, we know that you are a teacher who has come from God. For no one could perform the signs you are doing if God were not with him."

Jesus replied, "Very truly I tell you, no one can see the kingdom of God unless they are born again."

"How can someone be born when they are old?" Nicodemus asked. "Surely they cannot enter a second time into their mother's womb to be born!"

Jesus answered, "Very truly I tell you, no one can enter the kingdom of God unless they are born of water and the Spirit. Flesh gives birth to flesh, but the Spirit gives birth to spirit. You should not be surprised at my saying, 'You must be born again.' The wind blows wherever it pleases. You hear its sound, but you cannot tell where it comes from or where it is going. So it is with everyone born of the Spirit." (John 3 v 1-8)

To be "born again" (or "born from above") means to be "born of the Spirit". The Holy Spirit gives supernatural new birth and makes a man or woman a child of God; he gathers them into fellowship with God. This truth of being gathered into fellowship with God is wonderfully developed by Jesus as he speaks to his inner circle of apostles in John 14–16.

"If you love me, keep my commands. And I will ask the Father, and he will give you another advocate to help you and be with you for ever—the Spirit of truth. The world cannot accept him, because it neither sees him nor knows him. But you know him, for he lives with you and will be in you. I will not leave you as orphans; I will come to you. Before long, the world will not see me any more, but you will see me. Because I live, you also will live. On that day you will realise that I am in my Father, and you are in me, and I am in you. Whoever has my commands and keeps them is the one who loves me. The one who loves me will be loved by my Father, and I too will love them and show myself to them."

Then Judas (not Judas Iscariot) said, "But, Lord, why do you intend to show yourself to us and not to the world?"

Jesus replied, "Anyone who loves me will obey my teaching. My Father will love them, and we will come to them and make our home with them." (John 14 v 15-23)

When Jesus has died, risen, and ascended to the Father, he will ask the Father, and the Father will give to the disciples "another advocate", that is, another who will be to them what Jesus has been to them while he was on earth. Jesus has brought them into fellowship with himself, and through him, into fellowship with the Father.

The promised other advocate will do the same. What is more, unlike Jesus who was taken from them, this advocate will be doing his work in them, "for ever" (v 16): he is already "with" them in some sense, but from that future day onwards (the day of Pentecost) he will be "in" them (v 17). As he comes to them, Jesus himself will come back to them (v 18), and give them his eternal life (v 19).

Then, wonderfully, they will grasp what has happened (v 20): just as Jesus is "in" the Father (walking with him in unbroken fellowship and love), so they are "in" Jesus and he "in" them. That is to say, the advocate has drawn them in to the fellowship of eternal love of the Trinity. In answer to the question (v 22) as to what is special about all this (that is, what is unique here to the disciples that is not experienced by the world outside), Jesus replies: "Anyone who loves me will obey my teaching. My Father will love them, and we [Father and Son] will come to them and make our home with them" (v 23). The Father and the Son come by the Spirit to make the home of God with the believer. The believer is drawn into the eternal fellowship of the Trinity.

Jesus returns to this theme in his great prayer of John 17. After praying for himself (v 1-5) and his apostles (v 6-19), his prayer broadens out as he prays for those who will believe in him through the testimony of the apostles.

> My prayer is not for them alone. I pray also for those
> who will believe in me through their message, that all of
> them may be one, Father, just as you are in me and I
> am in you. May they also be in us so that the world
> may believe that you have sent me. I have given them
> the glory that you gave me, that they may be one as we
> are one—I in them and you in me—so that they may
> be brought to complete unity. Then the world will
> know that you sent me and have loved them even as
> you have loved me. (John 17 v 20-23)

The "oneness" and "unity" God gives believers by his Spirit is the ultimate gathering and the end to all scatterings. There is no gathering more secure or more long-lasting than the eternal fellowship of the Trinity, and believers are brought in to this circle of everlasting love. In a very deep sense, this is Eden restored.

## Questions for Discussion

1. Review the first section of this chapter. Why can the people of God not be reassembled until the Spirit of God is breathed into them?
2. Why can the Spirit not be given to live within people until after the Cross?
3. How did the day of Pentecost signal that the scattering of Babel was going to be reversed? How did this reversal begin to happen after that day?
4. What experience do you have of the Spirit of God bringing a spiritual unity between Christians?

# EIGHT

# Church: Gathered Worldwide

## God is Remaking the World through the Local Church

What do we think about, as we assemble with our local church, perhaps for a regular Sunday meeting? My guess is we mostly don't say to ourselves, "This rather mixed and motley gathering of strange men and women (I include myself!) contains within it the cure for a broken world." The thesis of this chapter, indeed the theme of the book, is precisely this: the ordinary local church, with all its imperfections, weaknesses, oddities and problems, has within it the seeds, the spiritual and relational genetic blueprint, of a broken world remade. Here at last is not just God restraining human strife, but God actively gathering. There is in the church not just a treatment delaying the onset of scattering, but a cure actively replacing scattering with gathering.

It does seem hard to believe, but I want to persuade us it is true. When once we are fully persuaded of this, our attitude to our local church will never be quite the same again. So let me stress again: this chapter is not about some theoretical or idealised local church; it is about the local church as it actually is, all over the world.

There have been some helpful books written about the local church.[57] I am not going to try to duplicate these books, but rather to focus on how the local church fits in to our Bible overview, how it is in the present God's actual realised remaking of a broken world. All over the world we will see God rebuilding, repairing, remaking; and we see it in local churches.

We shall also have to address some obvious and forceful objections: that religion is a divisive rather than uniting force in society; that Christian churches are endlessly splitting rather than harmonious—and indeed it is an observable fact on the ground that some local churches do the exact opposite of contributing to remaking a broken world. And yet I hope we shall end with a thoughtful and clear conviction that the thesis is true.

## The Local Church is a "Scattered Gathering"

We begin with a paradox. So far we have seen a consistent theme through the Bible: the judgment of God leads to scattering and he shows his grace and faithfulness by gathering. Adam and Eve were "scattered" from Eden in judgment for disobedience; the people at Babel were scattered as punishment for pride; Israel were gathered by God at Sinai and then again at Jerusalem, but scattered to Babylon in judgment. The Cross is the place of gathering, and Pentecost is the gathering reversing the scattering of Babel.

Yet we are now to see a scattering that turns out to be the outworking of God's grace rather than God's judgment. This paradox is anticipated at the Cross. When Jesus was arrested, the disciples "deserted him and fled" (Mark 14 v 50). Jesus knew this would happen and had told them it would be the fulfilment of a prophecy in Zechariah:

"This very night you will all fall away on account of me, for it is written:

'I will strike the shepherd, and the sheep of the flock will be *scattered*.'" (Matthew 26 v 31)

He had warned them "a time is coming and in fact has come when you will be *scattered*, each to your own home" (John 16 v 32). This scattering seemed to contradict Jesus' statement that on the Cross he would draw all kinds of people to himself (John 12 v 32): the exact opposite is the first thing that happened! And yet this terrible event, when the Shepherd who was promised to bring God's people together was killed and his followers scattered, turns out to be the key to a remade world.

The paradox continues after Pentecost: there is a great scattering that is the outworking of the faithfulness and rescue promises of God to gather a broken world. The days and weeks following Pentecost were filled with hostility to the church, culminating in the stoning of Stephen as the first martyr in Acts 7. Then we read:

And Saul approved of their killing him.

On that day a great persecution broke out against the church in Jerusalem, and all except the apostles were *scattered* throughout Judea and Samaria. (Acts 8 v 1)

This was not the scattering of God's enemies, but of God's friends. But let us see what happened, as we read ahead in Acts.

Now those who had been scattered by the persecution that broke out when Stephen was killed travelled as far as Phoenicia, Cyprus and Antioch, spreading the word only among Jews. Some of them, however, men from

Cyprus and Cyrene, went to Antioch and began to
speak to Greeks also, telling them the good news about
the Lord Jesus. The Lord's hand was with them, and a
great number of people believed and turned to the
Lord. (11 v 19-21)

As a result of the scattering of persecution, all sorts of unlikely
and distant people were gathered in to belong to the Lord!
Local churches began to be planted all over the world. Those
local churches are not "scatterings" of people under judgment:
they are "scattered gatherings", by which people all over the
world will be gathered in to Jesus. They are scattered in order
to reach the world; and they are gathered locally as signposts
to the final gathering of God's people at the end of time.

The Greek word translated "church" (*ecclesia*) means a
congregation or assembly of people gathered together. It is
the usual Greek word used to translate the Hebrew word for
the "assembly" of Israel, from "the day of the assembly" at
Mount Sinai onwards. The "assembly" of Israel is a kind of
prototype "church" (Acts 7 v 38, "the church in the wilderness", as the Authorised Version puts it). A local church is
also called a "synagogue", which also means a gathering and
is, of course, also used of the assemblies of Jewish people all
over the Diaspora (James 2 v 2, "meeting"). Similarly, Paul
uses the "synagogue" verb (*synago*) when he writes to the
church in Corinth: "When you are *assembled* [synagogued,
gathered together] … and the power of our Lord Jesus is
present" (1 Corinthians 5 v 4).

The Christian church is an assembly in the name of the Lord
Jesus. The local church is the concrete expression in this age of
the gathering by God of his people. It is the Temple of the Holy
Spirit, the place on earth where God lives, the community of

Jesus to which the Tabernacle in the desert and the Temple in Jerusalem pointed (1 Corinthians 3 v 9, 16; 1 Peter 2 v 5).

## The Local Church: Genetic Blueprint of a Remade World

We shall now explore seven elements of the genetic blueprint of a reassembled world, each of which is to be found in the authentic local church.

### A. Gathered by grace

The local church is an assembly for access to God by the death of Jesus. We have seen repeatedly (and especially in Chapters 1 and 2) that the fundamental reason why human relationships are so fragile and broken is that our fellowship with God has been broken by sin: that we are, in the language of Genesis 3, excluded from the garden of Eden. Access to God is therefore the precondition for the re-establishment of stable human harmony.

The Assembly of Israel at Sinai was an ambiguous anticipation of this access. Although the LORD "came down" and was present amongst his people, they were absolutely forbidden to draw near to him. It was an assembly at a distance. So let us go back to the passage in Hebrews 12 where the writer says Christian assemblies are coming to the heavenly Jerusalem rather than coming to Sinai (v 18-29). The writer of this letter is very keen to encourage his readers to keep on meeting. "Let us … not [give] up meeting together, as some are in the habit of doing, but [encourage] one another—and all the more as you see the Day approaching" (10 v 24-25).

One of the ways he encourages them near the end of his letter is to lift their eyes to understand what they are doing when they meet with their brothers and sisters. In this magnificent passage he contrasts the assembly at Sinai with the New Covenant assembly at "the heavenly Jerusalem". "You have not come to" Sinai, he says, with a vivid description of the sheer terror of that assembly (12 v 18-21). I take it that when the writer says, "You have not come … You have come…" (v 18, 22), he speaks of the heavenly assembly as it is expressed tangibly in our local church assemblies. He is not speaking just of individual Christians coming in some mystical way to the heavenly Jerusalem, but very concretely of their local church meetings. So, if a local church meeting is not terrifying like Sinai, what is it?

> But you have come to Mount Zion, to the city of the living God, the heavenly Jerusalem. You have come to thousands upon thousands of angels in joyful assembly, to the church of the firstborn, whose names are written in heaven. You have come to God, the Judge of all, to the spirits of the righteous made perfect, to Jesus the mediator of a new covenant, and to the sprinkled blood that speaks a better word than the blood of Abel. (12 v 22-24)

He is filled with joyful adoration because we have *not* come to Sinai. Thank God, he says, we have not come to that place of terror, distance and forbidden access.

However, in at least four ways the local church assembly *is* like Sinai, and we ought to note these before we look at the differences. First, it is still an assembly! Second, it is still an assembly in the presence of God (we come "to God, the Judge of all", v 23). Third, the God in whose presence we assemble is still "a consuming fire" (v 29), just as he always was and always will be. Fourth, we still assemble to hear and heed his word ("See to it that you do not refuse him who speaks," v 25).

But the place has moved (in Bible imagery) from Sinai to Zion, to the place where the blood of the Covenant has been shed, to the place where the mediator of a better Covenant welcomes us, takes us by the hand and brings us to God (1 Peter 3 v 18). This is now the place where we draw near with confidence. It is no longer a gathering for distance, but an assembly for access.

The key to the access available in this assembly is the contrast in Hebrews 12 v 24 between "the blood of Abel" and "the sprinkled blood that speaks a better word than the blood of Abel". The blood of Abel "cries out" from the ground for God to act in judgment upon Cain; it "speaks" by crying out for just judgment upon Cain and upon all sinners (Genesis 4 v 10). If the only "sound" God hears is the blood of Abel, then all of us are doomed to destruction. We cannot access a holy God without being burned alive by the consuming fire of his justice.

By contrast with this, "the sprinkled blood" reminds us of the blood of the covenant sacrifice sprinkled by Moses on the people (Exodus 24 v 6-8). It also reminds us of the blood of the Passover Lamb saving the firstborn from death: so "the church of the firstborn" (Hebrews 12 v 23) seems to refer back to the Passover. The Passover was also in the writer's mind in 11 v 28: "By faith [Moses] kept the Passover and the application of blood, so that the destroyer of the firstborn would not touch the firstborn of Israel'.

The "blood" of the Passover and the Covenant foreshadowed the death of a sacrifice in our place, and the "sprinkled blood" speaks of the benefits of that death being applied to us. The wonderful thing about the local church assembly is that it is the one "place" on earth where men and women can now have access to God as they gather in the name of Jesus and trust in his death for them. Now at last the cherubim can be stood down from their vital job as the "bouncers" on the door of the Garden of Eden; now a violent thief can be promised that on the day of his execution he will be with Jesus in the garden; now men and women can be reconciled to God and stand in the grace won for them by the Cross (Luke 23 v 43; Romans 5 v 1-11).

## B. Humbled under grace

Our self-perception as Christians deeply affects whether or not Christ builds an authentic church through us. Who I am determines the friends I make. That's a simple principle every teacher sees at work in the school playground: you see a teenager unsure of her identity, wandering unstably from group to group. Will she be a conformist or a rebel, with the trendy or the plain, the steady or the wild, the goths or the geeks? Then she makes her decision, and you know the decision she has taken because of the group to which she now belongs, where she hangs out. Who I am determines where I belong. Identity shapes community, self-perception forms fellowship. In order to be accepted by a social group I must line up my self and my identity with their character.

This simple principle holds not only in the playground, but with every human community, and it holds in the local church. The character of the local church is moulded by the self-perception of its members. Who we think we are individually will shape the fellowship we form and the people who join us.

East of Eden perhaps the most obvious cause of separation and scattering is pride. This is why when Jesus builds his church he must first destroy pride. Pride was the mindset of the builders of the Tower of Babel. The first thing that the gospel of the Cross does is to humble us deeply under grace. In a crucial passage in the letter to the Romans, Paul teaches them what Jesus did on the cross and how this makes it possible for guilty men and women to be in right relationship with God (Romans 3 v 21-26). Immediately after this, he tells them the "so what?" of this truth: "Where, then, is boasting? It is excluded" (v 27). In the context of Romans, the boasting in Paul's mind is probably the boasting of the religious person who thinks he or she is on a higher level than others in the church. But the point is simple: if the only way I can be reconciled to God is for Jesus to die for me, and if I am not able to make any contribution at all to my justification, it follows I had no cause of boasting, have no reason to boast, and can never ever have even the slightest reason to feel pleased with myself and superior to others. The pride of Babel is utterly undermined by the gospel of the Cross. There are no tower-builders in Eden.

Any gathering based upon anything we have done, any of our achievements, any of our privileges or any tribal markers of belonging, is doomed to scattering, because it is rooted in human pride. Those who belong to such a gathering do so because of some merit or privilege in them. It will therefore inevitably degenerate into what someone has called a "prig sty", a place for stuck-up prigs who are proud to belong. Such a community will always be riven with splits as one group and another, or one individual or another, make bids for supremacy and priority.

Another way of saying we are humbled under grace is to say we are to be "like children". In Matthew 16 Jesus says he is going to build his church, that is, to gather together his assembly (v 18). In Matthew 18 he speaks to his disciples about what kind of gathering they will be. Matthew 18 begins with a question about status: "Who ... is the greatest in the kingdom of heaven?" (v 1). This is not a question that has gone away in the history of the church: how can I use the church to gain status?

Before Jesus states anything, he calls for his visual aid, a child. He stands him in the middle of the disciples, pauses, and says, *I want you to grasp, because this is important, that unless you turn your attitudes 180 degrees around and become like children, you won't enter the kingdom. Never mind having status, you won't even get past the front door. But if you become like a kid then you will have real substantial status in the kingdom* (v 3-4).

What does Jesus mean by saying his followers must become "like little children"? He does not mean children are innocent. Some years ago I read a newspaper report in which police called at a house to arrest a teenager suspected of shoplifting. His mother and teenage sister said he wasn't at home. But his toddler brother blurted out, "Oh, yes, he is. He's hiding in the wardrobe!" The policeman commented later to the press that this showed "children that age can only tell the truth; and that is nice." Well, it would be nice, if it were true. But I can only conclude that that policeman was neither a father nor an uncle nor a teacher, nor had ever had anything to do with real children. Children are not innocent. Nor does Jesus mean that children are trusting. They may be; they may not. Kids can be deeply and healthily suspicious, especially of strangers. Nor does Jesus mean that, as one commentary claims, children are, "untempted to self-advancement". This is a strange idea and reminds me of the man who wrote in his autobiography, apparently unaware of the irony: "I have never lost the child-like humility which characterizes all truly great men."

No, the point about a child is not some supposed subjective virtue. It is the child is objectively, in terms of status and the perception of society, a nobody. The question Jesus was asked was about status; the answer he gives is about status. The child is to be looked after, not looked up to. The child is weak, yes, vulnerable, yes, and—in first century Jewish society—pretty much despised. Attitudes in Jesus' day would be more like that of Kingsley Amis, who said, "It was no wonder that people were so horrible, when they started life as children", or Nancy Mitford, who said, "I love children—especially when they cry, for then someone takes them away". You did not hold on to childhood in Jesus' culture, like Peter Pan: you longed to grow up, to become a full voting member of society, to be treated with respect, and so on.

So to turn and humble yourself like a child is not to take on the supposed sweet innocent self-effacing humble mind-set of the child: that is an imagined construction of the romantic mind. No, it is to accept the status of the child, to grasp and accept that I have no status. I am a nobody. I bring nothing with me into the kingdom. I must expect the world to look down on me, much as I would prefer it to look up.

This is what Jesus did. When Jesus humbled himself, he did not become innocent having previously been guilty; nor did he stop seeking advancement when he previously had; nor become trusting when he had formerly been suspicious (Philippians 2 v 8). Instead, he took the status of a despised human being, when he had previously lived in glory. He was born to an unmarried mother, hunted by Herod in infancy, an inhabitant of despised Nazareth (John 1 v 46; 7 v 41), baptized with sinners, followed by fishermen, with nowhere to lay his head, misunderstood and rejected by his own family, and finally hounded to a shameful and undeserved death.

Only the message of grace can so humble you and me that we cease to be driven by the divisive desire for status in the church. The desire for status divides and scatters. Only grace unites.

The story is told in the 1820s in England of a Holy Communion service in a village church, at which the Duke of Wellington was present. In those years after the battle of

Waterloo, the duke was the greatest citizen in the country under the king, sometime prime minister and a man of very great status. The expectation was the duke would take communion on his own first, and only then would the bread and wine be given to the rest of the congregation. But by some misunderstanding, a common farm worker found himself alongside the duke waiting for the bread and wine. The poor man was very embarrassed and made as if to return to his seat, when the duke motioned him to stay, and said, "We are all equal here". I don't know if the duke really said that, but if he did, he was absolutely right! The church of Jesus Christ ought to be a place where all desire for status and all arrogant scrambling for it, is eliminated by the gospel of the Cross. By this humbling a broken world will be remade.

## C. Inclusive by grace

A consequence of this humbling is that the authentic local church will welcome anyone, no matter what their race, education, culture or status in the eyes of the world. The logic is that we come into the kingdom as nobodies, and because we all know that we have no status we ourselves will willingly welcome other nobodies to join us. Or, to be precise, we will recognise that Jesus has already welcomed other nobodies to join us, and we will reflect his welcome in the welcome we too extend to them.

This logic is evident in the same passage in Matthew 18. Immediately after saying his disciples must "change and become like little children", Jesus says, "whoever welcomes one such child in my name welcomes me. If anyone causes one of these little ones—those who believe in me—to stumble, it would be better for them to have a large millstone hung around their neck and to be drowned in the depths of the sea" (v 4-6).

The "little one" is the same as the "child", a metaphor for the Christian of any age (hence the explanation "those who believe in me"). If we have not turned and become like children, accepting zero status, then we will treat applicants for membership in the way any human club treats applicants: we will ask if they can step up and meet the entrance requirements, if they qualify to belong. We will cause them to stumble at the church door, turning them away in our pride unless they are people like us.

But with Jesus it was so different: because Jesus had no status, he attracted to himself men and women who had no status. His group was defined by the negation of human status: therefore the least, the lost and the last were drawn to him like parched men to water.

When I walk in Jesus' footsteps and become "like a child" I will willingly receive a "child" into my group. Only when my self-perception is that I am a despised nobody will I welcome other despised nobodies into my fellowship. Only when I myself am deeply humbled will my door be open to the lost, the struggling and the desperate.

If we do not receive nobodies, we do not receive Jesus Christ. That is why putting up barriers of pride is so serious. That is why it would be better to have a quick and early death by drowning, with a millstone round our necks, than to put up barriers of pride (see Matthew 18 v 6). That is why it is so desperately important a church be a church of "children", a church in which status is zero and agreed to be zero and proclaimed to be zero.

This is so different to the religion of the Pharisees. In Matthew 23 Jesus condemns them for laying heavy burdens on the people. They get their praise from one another, the religious people. They get their status from their praying or their generous giving or their fasting, their zeal and public piety (as in Matthew 6). In particular, Jesus says to them that they shut the kingdom of heaven in people's faces (23 v 13), because (a) they themselves do not enter (they don't become like children), and therefore (b) they do not allow those who would enter to go in. That is to say, they won't become like children and therefore they won't receive "children". They put a stumbling block in the way. And so Jesus says the tax collectors and prostitutes go in to the kingdom before them (21 v 31), because these no-hopers grasp that they are nobodies and therefore exactly the people Jesus wants to gather.

The church of Jesus Christ is inclusive by grace. This is a hard thing to be, because it is so against the values of the world, and the world will despise us for it. By nature every human community is like an economic trade area that places a tariff barrier around it. You may join us, but only if you pay, only if you can manage the tariff. By nature every church is like this. We'd love you to join our club, but only if you become like us. But Jesus proclaims a community that undermines all tariff barriers. It is a community, a fellowship, with no moral tariff barrier to entry, a society with open doors to receive anyone who will turn and abandon self-righteousness, or pride in status, and come empty-handed to the foot of the Cross of Christ, and then be changed by grace.

The only person who will be excluded from the church is the one who thinks he or she has no need of grace. Only pride, or proud impenitence, can keep someone outside. The assembly of Jesus Christ has no step that someone has to step up to get in: but it has a very low gate, so that only those who abandon self-righteousness and status will bow low enough to come in. People are excluded not by being too low, but by thinking themselves too high. This welcoming inclusiveness of grace is the seed of a remade world.

Another place where this barrier-breaking dynamic of the local church is seen is Paul's letter to the Ephesians. The message of grace proclaims that we can contribute nothing at all to being rescued: it follows that anyone anywhere in the world can be rescued, and will be rescued only through the kindness of God in Jesus at the Cross. This message is not tied to one particular ethnic group, one language group, one social class or one culture.

> For he himself [Jesus] is our peace, who has made the two groups one and has destroyed the barrier, the dividing wall of hostility, by setting aside in his flesh the law with its commandments and regulations. His purpose was to create in himself one new humanity out of the two, thus making peace, and in one body to reconcile both of them to God through the cross, by which he put to death their hostility. He came and preached peace to you who were far away and peace to those who were near. For through him we both have access to the Father by one Spirit. (Ephesians 2 v 14-18)

It matters deeply that the local assembly of a Christian church does not exclude anyone on grounds of race, culture or class. To do so is a denial of the gospel of grace. There was a dramatic showdown over this issue very early in the life of the young Christian churches, in Antioch, the first city where the gospel was shared with Gentiles (Acts 11 v 20). Jews and Gentiles were, amazingly, eating together as a sign they had been brought together in Jesus by the Cross. But then a group of conservative Jews from Jerusalem arrived and started eating separately. Even the apostle Peter succumbed to pressure to eat separately, and Paul courageously challenged him, realising that the gospel itself was at stake.

When [Peter] came to Antioch, I opposed him to his face, because he stood condemned. For before certain men came from James, he used to eat with the Gentiles. But when they arrived, he began to draw back and separate himself from the Gentiles because he was afraid of those who belonged to the circumcision group. The other Jews joined him in his hypocrisy, so that by their hypocrisy even Barnabas was led astray.

When I saw that they were not acting in line with the truth of the gospel, I said to [Peter] in front of them all, "You are a Jew, yet you live like a Gentile and not like a Jew. How is it, then, that you force Gentiles to follow Jewish customs? We who are Jews by birth and not sinful Gentiles know that a person is not justified by the works of the law, but by faith in Jesus Christ. So we, too, have put our faith in Christ Jesus that we may be justified by faith in Christ and not by the works of the law, because by the works of the law no one will be justified." (Galatians 2 v 11-16)

To impose any kind of cultural bar to fellowship is "not acting in line with the truth of the gospel" (v 14) and must be stopped. The local church ought to be the one place in a society where the deepest divides begin to be bridged. But this cannot be achieved by social engineering, or by exhortation from church leaders: it happens only as the grace of God in Jesus is preached repeatedly and applied practically in every area of church life.

It is worth saying that we cannot make any of our churches perfectly multicultural. There are all sorts of reasons why our local churches will often tend to be dominated by one particular culture, not least because they are local and reflect the culture(s) of the localities in which they are placed (and, of course, they have to choose which language to conduct their meetings in). We must not beat ourselves up because our churches are not perfectly mixed. When Jesus builds his church he starts with very broken materials. The key is we are consciously and deliberately seeking to see the message of grace break down barriers. It is not so much where our churches have got to that matters, but what direction they are moving in.

## D. Connected by grace

I have spoken of the "local church". Some will wonder where a denomination fits in to the picture, such as the Church of England, the Baptist Union, or the Presbyterian Church of America, or an association, connection or fellowship of churches, such as the Fellowship of Independent Evangelical Churches. It is important to be clear that when the New Testament writers address "the church" in a particular place, they write to what we would call a local church (or possibly a small group of churches in the same locality). The word "church" in the New Testament usually means either a local church or the universal church (all people who belong to Christ, from every age and every place).

The local church recognises it is one of a large number of worldwide scattered gatherings. This means a strong awareness that no one local church stands alone. We are part of a global movement of God which is not aimed at just producing separate local gatherings, but will in the end lead to one worldwide people. Paul starts 1 Corinthians by writing, "to the church of God in Corinth", that is, he writes to one local gathering. But he goes on to describe them as "sanctified in Christ Jesus and called to be his holy people" (that is, set apart to belong to Christ and called to behave in a "set apart" way) "together with all those everywhere who call on the name of our

Lord Jesus Christ—their Lord and ours" (1 Corinthians 1 v 2). Wherever we gather, we are to remember our spiritual identity is shared with all those everywhere who call on the name of Jesus. Our experience will be different in detail, but similar in essentials to that of all Christians everywhere (see, for example, 1 Thessalonians 2 v 14; 1 Peter 5 v 9).

We ought not to be dogmatic about exactly how this awareness of worldwide fellowship will manifest itself in a local church. There are all sorts of ways, both formal and informal, in which this interlinked fellowship is expressed. But the important thing is an individual local church remembers that we are part of a much bigger movement of God, by which he will gather in men and women from all over the world into one flock under one Shepherd (John 10 v 16).

### E. Secure in grace

The local church is a people who are secure and satisfied in the God of grace. Like the Jerusalem of Old Testament promise, the church is the place of security in a broken world. James the brother of Jesus addresses the problem of quarrelling in a surprising way:

> What causes fights and quarrels among you? Don't they come from your desires that battle within you? You desire but do not have, so you kill. You covet but you cannot get what you want, so you quarrel and fight.
>
> (James 4 v 1-2)

Why do they quarrel? Because they covet and cannot get what they want. So what is the remedy for covetousness?

> You do not have because you do not ask God. When you ask, you do not receive, because you ask with

wrong motives, that you may spend what you get on
your pleasures. (v 2-3)

They quarrel because they covet and cannot have what they
want: they do not have because they do not ask God, and
even when they do ask God, they ask just so they can enjoy
their selfish pleasures. That is, they want to use God like a
magic wand to help them get what they want. James goes on
to say they need to repent and humble themselves before
God (4 v 4-10). Only when they learn to find their satisfaction in the grace God loves to pour out (v 6) will they learn
contentment.

In the same way, the writer to the Hebrews answers the love
of money with the promise and sufficiency of God.

Keep your lives free from the love of money and be
content with what you have, because God has said,
  "Never will I leave you;
    never will I forsake you." (Hebrews 13 v 5)

The authentic local church is a place where men and women
are beginning to learn to find their identity and security in the
God of promise and grace. This safe grace is the root answer to
human desires that lead to quarrelling, discontent and division.
In this way too the local church contains within itself the seeds
of a remade world.

### F. Forgiving through grace
The local church is an assembly able to stay together in harmony
because they forgive as the Lord forgave them. Forgiveness is a
vital element in the cure for scattering. The only safe dynamic
that can unlock unlimited forgiveness is the gospel of the
Cross. Paul writes to the Colossians:

> Therefore, as God's chosen people, holy and dearly loved, clothe yourselves with compassion, kindness, humility, gentleness and patience. Bear with each other and forgive one another if any of you has a grievance against someone. *Forgive as the Lord forgave you.*
>
> (Colossians 3 v 12-13)

We can only forgive freely when we know deeply that we have been forgiven freely. Few things divide and scatter human beings as deeply as unforgiveness. Many marriages end up being broken not by the bad behaviour of one party but by the refusal of the other to forgive. Only the gospel of free scandalous forgiveness can set us free to offer free scandalous forgiveness to others, and therefore to continue to live in fellowship with them in spite of their, and our, sinfulness.

Let us return to Matthew 18 and see how Jesus unlocks this dynamic in the parable of the unforgiving servant (v 21-35). It is a shocking passage, for at the end of it the person tortured for eternity is not an offender but a victim. A man who is wronged at the start (by an unpaid debt) ends up tortured at the end. This is such a horrifying scenario we had better look carefully at what is going on, because the Lord Jesus Christ teaches us this is how things will actually be.

The context of the parable is a block of teaching to the disciples (all of Matthew 18) in which Jesus teaches how he will build his church. We have seen that he first demolishes pride by teaching we must become "like little children". We must be nobodies, and welcome nobodies. Verses 15 to 20 address the problem when a believer sins and persistently will not repent. Now Jesus comes to the—in some ways harder—question of what to do if they sin and do repent, again and again! Each time they cause pain within the fellowship they repent, but they go on doing it.

That is Peter's question in verse 21. It is so typical of Peter to ask the question that needs to be asked. "Lord, how many times shall I forgive my brother or sister who sins against me?" The implication is that the Christian brother or sister does repent, because if they won't repent, then verses 15 to 17 tell us what to do. And in the closely parallel passage in Luke 17 v 3-4 Jesus says, "If your brother or sister sins against you, rebuke them; and if they repent, forgive them. Even if they sin against you seven times in a day and seven times come back to you saying, 'I repent,' you must forgive them." So the implication here is forgiveness can only effectively be offered and received by one who repents. But what are the limits of offered forgiveness? What if a brother or sister does repent?

In some ways this is even harder than if they don't. For our hearts are such that it is somehow gratifying to press on with the process of Matthew 18 v 15-17. When the door is finally shut on this impenitent offender and he is locked out of the fellowship, we feel he had it coming to him, he got his just deserts, and it served him right. There is something satisfying about that! Everyone can see I was the victim, and he was the offender, and now he is punished, as offenders should be.

But what if he repents? Well, of course I must forgive him the first time, and the second, and I guess, to stretch a point, the third. There was a tradition in the rabbis that three times was about right. But after that I must conclude that his repentance is not genuine, whatever he says, mustn't I? I can't go on forgiving. Peter is generous. How about "seven times" he suggests? That's a lot (and a biblical symbolic number of completeness), and it echoes Luke 17 v 4.

Jesus says, *Peter, I don't think you've understood the meaning of "seven". When I say that if he sins and repents seven times you must forgive him, I didn't mean "seven" as a mathematical number, but as a number that means "on and on and on".* We would say infinity. "I tell you, not seven times, but seventy-seven times"—or it may be seventy times seven, but the meaning is the same, on and on and on without limit (Matthew 18 v 22).

Seventy-seven is precisely how revenge works. In Chapter 1 we met Lamech with his boast of revenge: "If Cain is avenged seven times, then Lamech seventy-seven times" (Genesis 4 v 24). The word for "seventy-seven" in the Greek translation of the Old Testament is the same as the word Jesus uses here in Matthew 18 v 22. Jesus says he wants his church to be the place where the world's disproportionate retaliation is turned upside down and becomes outrageously disproportionate forgiveness. At the end of the parable (v 35) he says this is not an optional extra: unless this limitless heartfelt forgiveness is forthcoming, the heavenly Father won't forgive us. James says the same: "judgment without mercy will be shown to anyone who has not been merciful" (James 2 v 13).

However, the important point for the church is to grasp the logic of the extraordinary parable in Matthew 18 v 23-35. A servant owes his king "ten thousand bags of gold", or "talents". A few years before Jesus told this story, the total annual revenue of Galilee, Perea, Judea, Samaria and Idumaea, was about 800 talents. The amount this man owes the king exceeds the total money in circulation in the whole country at the time. "Ten thousand" was the biggest number in the Greek language; and the talent was the biggest unit of currency. So we might say, he owed the king trillions of pounds, dollars or euros. It is an astronomical debt. Astonishingly, the king releases him from this debt. The servant then meets a fellow servant who owes him "a hundred silver coins", or denarii. A denarius was about a day's wage for a labourer so this was not a trivial debt:

it was more than three months' wages.[58] The first servant will not forgive his debtor. We know the rest of the story: he is thrown into jail and held accountable for everything he owed the king.

The logic of the story is this: the only dynamic that will unlock forgiveness in human community is a deep understanding of the astronomical debt which God has forgiven us in Christ. It would be quite unreasonable to expect the servant to release his fellow-servant from a debt of three months' wages, *except that we know* that he himself had first been released from a debt of several hundred thousand years' worth of wages. Only the gospel of the Cross will bring this understanding deeply into our hearts: and therefore only the gospel of the Cross can unlock really costly and supernatural forgiveness of a kind able to really remake a broken world.

## G. Suffering through grace

The final mark I want to note by which the local church has the seeds of remaking a broken world is a surprising one: we exist and function in weakness rather than power. We are a society which follows a Master who suffered in weakness and refused to use power to defend himself, because the source of his kingly power was not worldly force. He said to Pontius Pilate, "My kingdom is not of this world", which means that the source of his authority was not from this world. "*If it were, my servants would fight* to prevent my arrest by the Jewish leaders" (John 18 v 36). Fighting, the exercise of all the power and force we can muster, is the way the world acts. But Jesus overcame evil with good and calls his followers to do the same (Romans 12 v 21). The local church is therefore to be a body of men and women who live in the world in weakness, who expect to be wronged and ill-treated, and who are learning not to hit back because they follow the one who, when he was insulted, did not retaliate, and when he suffered, made no threats (1 Peter 2 v 23).

This is an extraordinary way to behave, but it is the only way that can remake a broken world. This is quite different from the ways of Babylon: and yet the only force that can overcome Babylon is the force of weakness, the power of the Cross. Babylon has no answer to this. So often in human revolutions an injustice is overcome by the greater power of what turns into a greater injustice. When this happens, all that happens is that one evil is replaced by another evil. Evil can only be overcome by good. Only a people confident of the grace of God can entrust themselves, as Jesus did, to the God who judges justly (1 Peter 2 v 23).

## The Local Church is a Mixture of Jerusalem and Babylon

These seven marks of the authentic local church are indeed the genetic blueprint for reassembling a fractured world. A society which is gathered by grace, humbled under grace, inclusive under grace, secure in grace, connected worldwide by grace, forgiving by grace and willing to suffer in grace will be a powerful force for harmony. They would be Jerusalem on earth in all her beauty.

Sadly, however, we have to recognise that every actual local church on earth is a mixture of Jerusalem and Babylon. If a church is defined and driven by the word of God preached in the power of the Spirit, then we may expect all these seven wonderful marks to be evident. But they will be evident in the midst of all the contradictory markers of Babylon. Humility will be mixed with pride, harmony spoiled by division, security undermined by people trying to prove themselves, connectedness undone by a parochial defensiveness, forgiveness neutered by resentments, and weakness replaced by worldly power-plays.

Real Christianity can become debased and become nothing better than any human religion. The history of Christian denominations seeking institutional unity epitomises this problem. An article describing a proposed reunification of two branches of the Russian Orthodox church commented that the disputes that lay behind the split they were seeking to heal were, "only one example of a paradox in the recent history of [Christianity]. Almost every time two Christian communities—split by politics, race, culture or doctrine—decide to reunite, a new division is created by those who cannot accept the merger."[59] Real Christian churches are not Jerusalem here on earth!

So we need to consider the kinds of way in which the authentic grace-shaped gathering of the local church can be replaced by some kind of pseudo-church, that calls itself church but is actually not the genuine article. There are plenty of gatherings both in the Bible and in human history that are counterfeit imitations of the spiritual gathering of the people of God. In their different ways they all take us back to Babel. Let us consider some of them.

### A. Counterfeit church: the idolatrous assembly

Even while the people of Israel were assembled by God at Sinai, they managed to transform their assembly from one of true worship into one of idolatry.

> When the people saw that Moses was so long in coming down from the mountain, they gathered round Aaron and said, "Come, make us gods…" (Exodus 32 v 1)

This was a kind of assembly (they "gathered round Aaron"). But it was not an assembly gathered by and under the word of God. On the contrary, it was an assembly of human initiative called in order to produce some gods shaped by human imagination. Any religious gathering not shaped week by week by the preaching of the word of God will revert to becoming an idolatrous assembly, in which human tradition or imagination will begin to shape gods made in our image. One of the tests of an authentic gospel assembly is the questions it asks when it wants to call or appoint a new pastor or leader. Do they ask, "Preach to us the word God has spoken"? Or is their agenda actually that he will work with them to produce a god shaped the way they would like God to be, perhaps the therapeutic god whose mission is to meet my needs and make me feel better?

Any "church" that in practice worships a god shaped by human desires will be a divisive rather than a uniting force in society, for it will inevitably be shaped by its own longings in a way that will bring it into conflict with other societies or communities, shaped in turn by their own prejudices, interests or desires.

## B. Counterfeit church: the self-righteous assembly

The prophets in the Old Testament sometimes looked at the gatherings of Israel and observed that they did nothing to change people's lives. These people met together in the name of God (we would call them a "church"), but there was no inner life-changing reality to correspond to what they said. They had "the form of godliness" but denied "its power" (2 Timothy 3 v 5). Of this kind of empty gathering, that just makes religious people feel better about themselves, God says:

I cannot bear your worthless assemblies. (Isaiah 1 v 13)

Your assemblies are a stench to me. (Amos 5 v 21)

This kind of "church" always metamorphoses into a church of Pharisees. If my life is not being changed by the word of God in daily repentance and fresh faith, the alternative is that I will be affirmed in my sinfulness and just end up feeling better and better about myself. This will always make me look down on others, and make the "church" a divisive force in society. Only when the church consists of men and women being humbled and changed by grace will it be the kind of society that welcomes other needy people in.

## C. Counterfeit church: the homogeneous assembly

The third kind of gathering that may look like a Christian church but is not, is an assembly that defines itself by some homogeneous cultural boundaries. It is clear, for example, from Galatians or Ephesians, that Paul would not have recognised as a church any assembly that defined itself as either Jewish or Gentile and did not allow the other category of person to belong, and indeed welcome them. What happens then is that a church metamorphoses into a club.

In some circumstances there is nothing wrong with a club. A sports club will welcome into membership those who play that sport, for example. In some way a club is defined by human talents (e.g. sport), human achievement (e.g. the wealth to pay the subscription) or human culture (e.g. a club for expatriates from one country in another). But a church is not a club. A church by definition welcomes any man or woman who will accept the free grace of God. A church must welcome a penitent murderer, a repentant member of a despised race or nation and a dropout and morally messed-up person who comes to his senses in the far country and returns to the Father God (Luke 15 v 11-24).

## D. Counterfeit church: the hostile assembly

Finally, the Bible observes a consistent pattern that one of the few things that will unite men and women without God is having God as their common enemy! In Numbers 16 Korah and his followers "banded [assembled] together" not because they were gathered by God but precisely "against the LORD" (Numbers 16 v 11). Psalm 2 pictures a great international alliance against God and his anointed Christ:

> The kings of the earth rise up
>> and the rulers band together
>> against the LORD and against his anointed [Messiah,
>> Christ]. (Psalm 2 v 2)

The anti-God archetypal alliance of Psalm 2 is fulfilled in the united hostility against Jesus. Immediately after quoting this psalm the disciples go on to say:

> Indeed Herod and Pontius Pilate met together with the Gentiles and the people of Israel in this city to conspire against your holy servant Jesus, whom you anointed [i.e. the Messiah of Psalm 2 v 2]. (Acts 4 v 27)[60]

In New Testament times King Herod wasn't generally friends with anyone, and yet paradoxically he found himself ganging up both with the Pharisees and later with Pontius Pilate against Jesus:

> Then the Pharisees went out and began to plot with the Herodians how they might kill Jesus. [Mark 3 v 6; and see also Mark 12 v 13 for the same surprising alliance.]

> That day [when Jesus was on trial] Herod and Pilate became friends—before this they had been enemies.
>> (Luke 23 v 12)

The same Psalm 2 anti-Christ alliance is precisely what the disciples face under persecution in Acts 4:

> The next day the rulers, the elders and the teachers of
> the law met in Jerusalem. Annas the high priest was
> there, and so were Caiaphas, John, Alexander and others
> of the high priest's family. (v 5-6)

Right through the story of Acts, the most bitter hostility to the gospel of grace comes from religious people, whether they be jealous Jews in the synagogues who feared the loss of religious power and influence, or pagan idolaters.[61]

## Conclusion: Persevere with the Mixed Experience of the Local Church

One of the paradoxes of contemporary culture is that two apparently contradictory things are often said about religion. On the one hand, it is frequently said that all religions are essentially the same. I am told that somewhere near Chicago there is a Bahai temple in which there is a central altar, from which nine aisles radiate like the spokes of a wheel from the hub. At the end of each aisle there is a little archway and each archway is dedicated to a different religious leader, each representing one of the world's religions. It doesn't matter which archway you enter through—basically you are doing the same thing and going to the same place.

And yet people also say religion is a very divisive influence in the world. But here's a puzzle: if religions are basically the same, how come they are so divisive? Or, to put it the other way, if they are so divisive, how come they haven't recognised they are all the same? The answer is that at a deep level they are all the same: but their sameness is "Tower of Babel" sameness rather than gospel sameness! Of course, there are enormous differences between the world's religions: for example, Buddhists do not really believe in god at all, whereas Hindus believe in many gods and goddesses. But beneath these differences they all affirm human initiative in religion and therefore puff up human pride. They are not rescue religions, religions of pure grace. At the centre of that Bahai temple there ought not to be an altar (symbolising access to God), but a boxing ring, since all that happens when human religions collide is strife. Only the gospel of pure grace can humble human beings and gather them together in love.

The assembly of the local church can so easily degenerate into being just a manifestation of another human religion yet carrying the "Christian" label. When a church degenerates like this it will usually show elements of some or all of these counterfeit assemblies. We must be realistic about this. And yet in the midst of all this disappointment we must not lose sight of the wonderful fact that where the gospel of grace is preached, the seven marks of a community that will rebuild a broken world will also be found.

If therefore we can join, belong and serve in such a fellowship, we will do well to do so. We will find ourselves to be a part of God's supernatural international plan to rebuild a broken world. The precise ways in which we serve as a part of this plan will vary enormously. For most Christians it will be a case of just belonging and serving wholeheartedly in a local church shaped by the word of God. Some will be sent out as missionaries in other cultures, or indeed in their own culture (perhaps as teachers in schools where they can reach others for Christ), and the constraints of their missionary work will limit their immediate involvement in a local church: but always they will have their eyes on the aim of seeing local churches built, men and women not just made into individualistic disciples but integrated into local church life as soon as possible. For a few, service of the local church may mean involvement in some para-church movement such as Christian Unions in schools or universities: but again, those of us who do this will always make sure that our para-church involvement really is serving the local church rather than seeking to upstage or replace it—for it is the local church, these wonderful scattered gatherings, which God is using to rebuild a broken world. In our final chapter we will lift our sights to see where the local church is heading.

## Questions for Discussion

1. In this chapter, how do we see God use the terrible scattering of persecution to bring about gathering of peoples from all over the world?

2. What seven elements did we note of the genetic blueprint of a reassembled world?

3. How can we make sure we are churches humbled under grace, and avoid worldly hierarchies and seeking after status? How do concerns about status creep into church life?

4. In particular, how can we honour the role of church leaders without giving them worldly status?

5. Review the section "Inclusive by grace". What should be the criterion used to decide whether or not someone is welcomed into a church fellowship? What other criteria do we mistakenly use?

6. What are the differences (in terms of human relationships) between a church splitting because of disagreements and a church sending out missionaries or a church-planting team? How do these differences show the difference between scattering as a sign of God's judgment and the creation of new "scattered gatherings"?

7. How can our churches build a sense of being part of a worldwide movement of God to remake a broken world?
8. How can we model a joyful contentment in God in the midst of an insecure world?
9. Think carefully to see if there are any people whom you need to forgive and have not forgiven, even though they have repented. Take to heart what Jesus teaches about how much God has forgiven you, and offer them forgiveness.
10. How do worldly attitudes towards wielding influence in society creep into Christian circles? How can we make sure we overcome evil only with good, and use the power of weakness rather than worldly strength?
11. Review the four types of counterfeit assembly we noted in this chapter. What warning signs might there be that a church is becoming one of these? How can we guard against this happening?

# The New Creation: Gathering Consummated

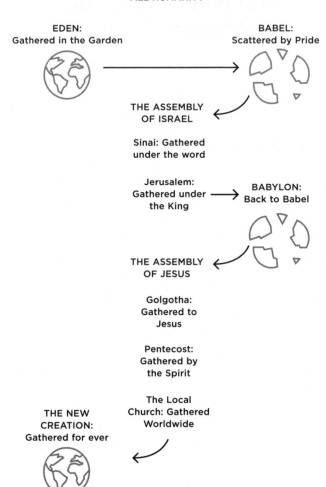

ALL HUMANITY

EDEN:
Gathered in the Garden

BABEL:
Scattered by Pride

THE ASSEMBLY
OF ISRAEL

Sinai: Gathered
under the word

Jerusalem:
Gathered under
the King

BABYLON:
Back to Babel

THE ASSEMBLY
OF JESUS

Golgotha:
Gathered to
Jesus

Pentecost:
Gathered by
the Spirit

The Local
Church: Gathered
Worldwide

THE NEW
CREATION:
Gathered for ever

# NINE

# The New Creation: Gathered Forever

## God's Master Plan

Near the start of his letter to the Ephesians, the Apostle Paul tells us something of great importance and wonder. He introduces it with a sustained build up: "[God] made known to us [the apostles] the mystery of his will"—that is, what he wanted and had decided to do, which had been hidden in Old Testament types and shadows, but has now been revealed —"according to his good pleasure"—this is what is really close to his heart—"… to be put into effect when the times reach their fulfilment" (Ephesians 1 v 9). It is quite a build up! So what is this decision and plan of God, known in shadowy form in the Old Testament, revealed clearly to the apostles and for us in the New Testament, and waiting to be finalised at the end of time? It is "to bring unity to all things in heaven and on earth under Christ" (v 10). What God has decided to do, longs to do, and most certainly will do at the end of time, is to gather together a broken world and rebuild it under one leader, the Lord Jesus Christ. This finally will be the keeping of the promise to Abraham that through his descendant he would rule the world and inherit the earth. This is the fulfilment of all those prophecies, such as Ezekiel 34–37, that God would put one shepherd, his servant David, over one united flock (see p 147-151).This at last will be the gathering to end all scatterings; and it will be cosmic in its scope.

Some while ago my family gave me a wonderful spherical jigsaw for my birthday. It was made of 500 rigid plastic curved pieces, and it made the globe of the world, painted with seas and countries, mountains, trade routes, longitude and latitude lines, and so on. We started with the pieces strewn over the floor, broken and scattered. My daughter and daughter-in-law helped me put it together: the feeling of satisfaction when we slipped the North Pole into place at the end was terrific: we had remade a broken globe! It had been scattered, and we had gathered it. I guess that feeling of delight is just a very pale echo of the glorious delight God will have on that day when he finally brings all things in heaven and on earth together under Jesus Christ. That is our subject in this final chapter.

## The Bible in three acts

We saw at the start that the Bible story can be told in three acts. Act I (Genesis 1–2) is the original created harmony of heaven and earth, one coherent creation, where the will of God is done equally on earth and in heaven and there is no divide or curtain between the two. Act II (most of the rest of the Bible story) recounts the separation of earth from heaven and the consequent fractures on earth, the Babel principle splitting human community like an old pane of glass shattering into thousands of pieces: but it also recounts the determination and plan of God to reinvade earth from heaven, to reconnect earth to heaven, and therefore to remake that broken world. We come now to Act III, the New Creation, the new heavens and new earth, the new Jerusalem.

## *Reemphasising a neglected truth*

My aim in this chapter is to bring a neglected Christian truth back into the forefront of our thinking, and by so doing to inspire us with the majesty of where the ordinary local church is heading. Some years ago we celebrated my father's ninetieth birthday and had a photographer to record the occasion. A photographer needs to be a bit bossy to get the family group in order. Sometimes someone very important has got lost at the back, perhaps a much-loved granny hidden behind a tall grandson, and the photographer has to say, "Granny, you are too important to be scarcely visible at the back; come and sit at the front." In the same way, the doctrine of this chapter is a senior doctrine in the Christian family photograph, but has sometimes got a bit lost at the back. It is the doctrine we affirm whenever we say in the Apostles' Creed, "I believe in … the resurrection *of the body*."

## *The glory of God spoiled on earth now*

Before we think about the reunification of heaven and earth, it is helpful to consider what is going on, on earth now and in heaven now, before reunification, rather as a book about contemporary Germany would need to cover both East Germany and West Germany in order to understand the meaning of reunification. We begin with earth now.

The most important reason we need to study the doctrine of the New Creation is the glory of God. Earth is under rebel rule. It is governed, in a sense, by the prince of this world; cut adrift from the good government of God through obedient human beings, it is a mess of conflicting power structures. There are spiritual forces of evil expressing themselves in political oppression, in injustice, and in personal slaveries to addictions, resentments, unforgiveness, greed and self-aggrandisement.

Because it is under a disordered rule, it gathers to itself its own glory. When the devil offers Jesus in the temptations, "the kingdoms of the world and their splendour", he is offering him stolen goods (Matthew 4 v 8). The whole creation is to be the theatre of God's glory. Whenever a human being, a family, a society, a government or a human project takes to itself glory, when I say, "Well done me!", or you say "Well done you!", or we say "Well done us!", we steal what is properly God's alone. When we speak of a "nature" programme, with no reference to the creator, this is a thieving of the glory of God.

A fractured earth governed by fighting ambitious human beings is not the theatre of God's glory as it ought to be. It is like a stage obscured by dry ice swirling around. In heaven there is glory; but on earth only echoes and footprints. A beautiful world has become a beautiful ruin.

So the question that ought to concern us is this: what happens to the glory of God? The creator God embarked on this project of making a good, very good, heavens and earth as the theatre of his glory: so what happens now? Is he to be frustrated by evil? Is his project to be finally spoiled, as a toy model might be ruined by a spiteful brother, spoiled and broken so it cannot be repaired and has to be thrown away with sadness? Or a beautiful garden graffitied and vandalised beyond repair, so that it has to be completely abandoned, and the gardener has to start somewhere else in defeat? Is that what happens to the glory of God? That is the big question.

The answer is: God wins, God remakes his broken world, and all the glory goes to God alone. The boy will rebuild his broken model; the gardener will restore his vandalised garden; the creator will remake his broken world.

*Who is in heaven now?*

If earth is spoiled, what is going on in heaven (which is God's "space" as opposed to our "space")? The New Testament teaches us at least four answers to the question, "Who is in heaven now?"

God the Father is there. He is "your Father in heaven", "your heavenly Father" (Matthew 5 v 45, 48). His will is done perfectly there ("as it is in heaven", Matthew 6 v 10). From there he has perfect knowledge of what happens on earth ("Your Father, who sees what is done in secret" and "knows [what] you need", Matthew 6 v 4, 32). It is true there are "spiritual forces of evil in the heavenly realms" (Ephesians 6 v 12), but above them, at a higher level of authority, there is a space in which the Father's will is perfectly done: it is the throne room of the universe.[62]

Second, since the Ascension, Jesus Christ is in heaven, in his resurrection body. He has "ascended to the Father" (John 20 v 17), "gone into heaven" (1 Peter 3 v 22), "entered heaven itself", where he has "sat down at the right hand of God" (Hebrews 9 v 24, 10 v 12); and there at the Father's right hand he rules with "all authority ... in heaven and on earth" (Matthew 28 v 18). We cannot understand how he can be there in bodily form, in a "place" that is inaccessible to our space-time universe, but it is important he is.

The bodily presence of Jesus in heaven shows us that heaven does not mean a non-material place ("spiritual" in the Greek sense of immaterial). This idea comes from ancient Greek philosophical dualism, that opposes the world of matter and material with the world of "spirit". This kind of unbiblical thinking keeps rearing its ugly head. For example, in Eckhart Tolle's very popular New Age book *A New Earth* he has a page head-ed "A new heaven and a new earth" in which he writes:

> The inspiration for the title of this book came from a
> Bible prophecy that seems more applicable now than at
> any other time in human history. It occurs in both the
> Old and the New Testament and speaks of the collapse of
> the existing world order and the arising of "a new heaven
> and a new earth". We need to understand here that heav-
> en is not a location but refers to the inner realm of con-
> sciousness. This is the esoteric meaning of the word, and
> this is also its meaning in the teachings of Jesus. Earth,
> on the other hand, is the outer manifestation in form,
> which is always a reflection of the inner. Collective
> human consciousness and life on our planet are intrinsi-
> cally connected. "A new heaven" is the emergence of a
> transformed state of human consciousness, and "a new
> earth" is its reflection in the physical realm.[63]

This is completely wrong! Heaven is a location. It is not a location within our space-time universe, but it is a location, a place other than our individual or collective consciousness. It is not found by going inside ourselves, but by belonging to Jesus who lives there in his resurrection body.

Third, it would seem dead Christians are in heaven in spirit. They are spoken of as being asleep (1 Thessalonians 4 v 13, rather as Jesus described Lazarus as being "asleep" in John 11 v 11), which seems to be a way of telling us their state is temporary, rather than telling us whether or not they are conscious; the New Testament is more interested in telling us about their future (bod-ily resurrection, when they "awake") than the precise details of their present state. It is enough that they are with Jesus: they are "with me where I am" (John 17 v 24). They are "with Christ, which is better by far" (Philippians 1 v 23). They are with Jesus, like the penitent thief on the cross, now "in paradise" (which would seem here to mean the place where the spirits of dead believers live temporarily with Jesus). There are "many rooms" in the Father's house, and believers are assured of a home there (John 14 v 2). They are not there in body (for their bodies are rotting or have been cremated or destroyed); but they are there in spirit. So it is true that when we die we go to heaven, in spirit but not in body, and temporarily, not forever.

Finally, living Christians are there in status. Their citizenship is in heaven: this is where they now belong (Philippians 3 v 20). In this sense they are "seated ... with [Christ] in the heavenly realms" (Ephesians 2 v 6). So although they live on earth, here they are "foreigners and exiles" (1 Peter 2 v 11). The treasure or inheritance of living Christians is kept safely in heaven. They have "treasures in heaven", an "inheritance ... kept in heaven" (Matthew 6 v 20, 19 v 21; 1 Peter 1 v 4). "Every spiritual blessing" is theirs "in the heavenly realms" (Ephesians 1 v 3). And the Holy Spirit on earth is "the guarantee of our inheritance until we acquire possession of it" (Ephesians 1 v 11-14 ESV). Heaven is like the safe in which our treasure and inheritance is guarded. And the Holy Spirit is like the title deed or deed of ownership of that inheritance.

## Heaven is not the end of the story

From time to time I used to take a very short train journey from Wimbledon in south-west London in to Waterloo, one of the central London termini. The journey lasts less than twenty minutes. Sometimes the following announcement is made over the intercom: "Thank you for travelling with South West Trains. We are now approaching Waterloo, *which is our final destination.*" It feels to me a little over the top somehow, almost apocalyptic, this talk of "final destinations". But it also seems a bit sad. I look around at my fellow passengers and hope the station is not their final destination. I hope they are travelling on to somewhere more interesting!

Heaven is not the final destination of Christian believers. It is a wonderful place, because it is with Jesus, which is far, far better than the troubles of this age (and a great deal better than Waterloo station). But it is not the end of the story. In fact, the New Testament is much more interested in what lies beyond heaven, than with heaven itself. It is true "our citizenship is in heaven" and our "inheritance that can never perish, spoil or fade" is "kept in heaven for" us (Philippians 3 v 20, 1 Peter 1 v 4). But we do not expect to enjoy that inheritance in heaven. Rather, *from heaven* "we eagerly await a Saviour … the Lord Jesus Christ, who, by the power that enables him to bring everything under his control, will transform our lowly bodies so that they will be like his glorious body" (Philippians 3 v 20-21). We expect Jesus to come from heaven bringing our promised inheritance with him to earth. Again, when Paul writes to the church in Philippi that he is confident God will carry on until he has finished his work in the church, he expects God to finish that work, not when they die and go to heaven, but at "the day of Christ Jesus", which means the day of his return and the bodily resurrection (Philippians 1 v 6). Paul is not longing finally to go to heaven, wonderful though that will be: he is reaching forwards to "the resurrection from the dead", which means the resurrection of the *body* (Philippians 3 v 11).

In the beatitudes from the Sermon on the Mount, Jesus promises that those who are persecuted for his sake will have a great reward "in *heaven*", but equally the meek "will inherit the *earth*" (Matthew 5 v 5, 12). He is not making separate promises in the beatitudes, as if those who pass the meekness test will be given the earth while those who are persecuted will go to heaven (and what happens to those who qualify on both counts?). Rather, he is giving the blessings that go with all the qualities of real godliness and genuine discipleship. There will be no difference between a reward in heaven and inheriting the earth, for the deep and simple reason that on that great day heaven and earth will be recombined!

In the apocalyptic language of Revelation, the souls of the martyrs do not say, *Well, this is nice; now we're in heaven, so that's OK*; no, they call out "in a loud voice, 'How long, Sovereign Lord, holy and true, until you judge the inhabitants of the earth and avenge our blood?'" (Revelation 6 v 10). That is to say, they have a forward focus, longing for the final judgment and the resurrection of the dead.

This forward longing has been expressed in Christian history on gravestones and memorial tablets. For example, in the church of St Andrew the Great in Cambridge there is a memorial to two boys who died aged eleven and twelve. It describes them as having died "in hope of a blessed resurrection". I came across an even more vivid example in Poets' Corner in Westminster Abbey, a place where a number of famous literary figures are buried. I was looking around feeling rather gloomy at the memorials to some notorious unbelievers like Oscar Wilde, when I stumbled upon this, to the sixteenth century poet Edmund Spencer:

> HEARE LYES (EXPECTING THE SECOND COMMINGE OF OUR SAVIOVR CHRIST JESUS) THE BODY OF EDMOND SPENCER THE PRINCE OF POETS IN HIS TYME WHOSE DIVINE SPIRRIT NEEDS NOE OTHIR WITNESSE THEN THE WORKS WHICH HE LEFT BEHINDE HIM. HE WAS BORNE IN LONDON IN THE YEARE 1553 AND DIED IN THE YEARE 1598.

I nearly danced around the Abbey singing hallelujah! Here was one poet, at least, who died looking forward to that great day, the second coming of our saviour Christ Jesus. This is authentic Christian hope. This is why we pray the corporate prayer, "Your kingdom come" in the Lord's Prayer, rather than the individual prayer, "Please take me to heaven."

Even Jesus Christ is looking forward to that great day. The letter to the Hebrews tells us that after the Cross, Jesus "sat down at the right hand of God". But he did not sit down and relax, if we may put it reverently. No, "Since that time he *waits* for his enemies to be made his footstool…" (Hebrews 10 v 12-13). Even Jesus in heaven waits for the day when heaven can be reunited with earth. His kingdom may not be "of this world" but is "from another place" (i.e. it does not derive its authority from this fallen world but from the Father in heaven); nevertheless, his kingdom will be *over* this world, as we shall see (John 18 v 36).

So we must consider the hope for which living Christians wait, dead Christians wait, and even Jesus waits. This is why the New Testament speaks primarily not of two places (earth here and heaven above) but of two ages, of "this age or the age to come" (Matthew 12 v 32; see also Ephesians 1 v 21), of "the end of the age" (Matthew 13 v 40, 49), after which "the righteous will shine like the sun in the kingdom of their Father" (v 43). The Father will rule his kingdom not in heaven alone, but in the whole universe, over a reunited heavens and earth. The letter to the Hebrews speaks of "the world to come" which will finally be under human rule, as it was always meant to be. It also speaks of "the powers of the coming age" (Hebrews 2 v 5; 6 v 5). The expression "eternal life" in John's Gospel is probably best understood to mean, "the life of the age to come", which means life in relationship with the Father and the Son (John 17 v 3). Jesus spoke of "the renewal of all things" (literally, "the regeneration"), which is the new birth of the whole cosmos (Matthew 19 v 28).

All this means we may need to reinterpret some of the language we use when we speak of heaven. We need to remember that heaven sometimes serves as a shorthand for "the New Creation". There is a rousing popular song in which we sing, "There's a place where the streets shine with the glory of the Lamb. There's a way; we can go there; we can live there beyond time".[64] Strictly speaking, I think we ought to sing, "There's a place where the streets shine with the glory of the Lamb. But we won't go there; it will come to us!"

### The New Jerusalem

In his letter to the Galatians Paul speaks of "the Jerusalem that is above" who is the spiritual "mother" of Christians; and the writer to the Hebrews says we "have come to Mount Zion, to the city of the living God, the heavenly Jerusalem" (Galatians 4 v 26; Hebrews 12 v 22). This new or heavenly Jerusalem is the spiritual reality to which the Old Testament Jerusalem pointed and which the local church anticipates. We should therefore expect it to express the realisation (the "making real or concrete") of the gathering of God. It does this in two ways.

First, it is the final gathering of all the people of God of every age. John describes a visionary anticipation of this in his famous words:

> After this I looked, and there before me was a great multitude that no one could count, from every nation, tribe, people and language, standing before the throne and before the Lamb. (Revelation 7 v 9)

This is the gathering anticipated on the first Christian Pentecost, where Babel began to be reversed and where the scattered human race began to be remade. Now at last it will be consummated forever and it will happen because they are gathered "before the throne [of God] and before the Lamb". As Paul says, the Christian hope is "the coming of our Lord Jesus Christ *and our being gathered to him*" (2 Thessalonians 2 v 1). We are gathered to one another because—and only because—we are gathered to Jesus.

Second, it will also represent the regathering or reconnection of heaven and earth. When John finally sees the new Jerusalem at the end of Revelation, he sees it "coming down out of heaven from God" (21 v 2, 10). The great section from Revelation 21 v 1 through to Revelation 22 v 5 describes this beautiful city as the Bride of Christ, as the place where God lives with his people forever (so there is no need for a Temple). This is the time when the garden of Eden reoccupies the earth, so that the tree of life is there. This is when Eden is restored to the whole earth. The city is about the size of the entire known world;[65] this would seem to symbolise that this wonderful city extends throughout the New Creation. To be in the new heavens and the new earth is to be in the New Jerusalem, or at least to have free access in and out of its gates (Revelation 21 v 25).

When we try to understand this New Creation, we need to be very careful to be guided by what we are told in the New Testament, and to resist the temptation to try to tie up all the loose ends and answer all our questions. But I think we may make five clear statements about the New Creation, as follows.

### 1. The New Creation is real and physical

There is significant continuity between the present age and the New Creation of the age to come. The New Creation is a "spiritual" place populated by "spiritual" bodies. But this does not mean it is immaterial. When Paul speaks of the resurrection body as being a "spiritual body", he means a body patterned on the resurrection body of Jesus (1 Corinthians 15 v 44). This was a physical body, one that could eat, be seen and touched (Luke 24 v 36-43). No doubt Jesus had a transformed physicality (he could come through a closed door, for example), but he was not ethereal, vague, immaterial or floating around: he was and is real. His body was "spiritual" because it belonged to the age of the Spirit and not to the present age of corruption and decay.

In Romans 8 Paul writes of the creation waiting "in eager expectation"; it has been "subjected to frustration", the miserable processes of death and decay. But it "will be liberated from its bondage to decay" and be brought into "freedom". It is "groaning"; but its groaning is not the misery of death throes, of knowing it will be cast upon the cosmic scrap heap. Rather, its groaning is "as in the pains of childbirth": this pain will lead to a new birth, the regeneration of the cosmos, and great joy (Romans 8 v 18-22). Creation does not groan because it knows its time is short and it will soon be destroyed: it groans like a mother-to-be enduring labour pains; its pain is suffused with hope. This is because it is not going simply to be replaced by an entirely discontinuous and non-physical order. It is not the case that the creation watches as Christians die and are transferred to heaven, knowing that when they have all gone, it will itself be doomed to destruction. Far from it: the creation longs to be set free from bondage. The creation is not a prisoner on death row, but a prisoner awaiting release. The voice John hears in Revelation 21 does not say, "I am making all new things", but "I am making all things new" (v 5 ESV): we expect a regeneration, not a simple replacement, of this cosmos.

This ensures that God wins. God made a good universe. That universe has been spoiled, but God has not given up on it: he does not say, "Well, that was a pity; I'd better start again". No, he will end the story with a good, real, physical cosmos that is the completion and perfection of his original creation. Nothing can stop him doing it.

The physical delight we may experience in the beauty of music, the stimulus of sport, the intimacy of sex within marriage, the taste of good food, the wonders of travel—all these will be there in transformed and transcended form in the New Creation. They will not be the same: for example, there will be no marriage (Matthew 22 v 30). But all the good delights human beings experience will be transcended and exceeded in that new age. No believer who "misses out" on any delight in this age will miss out for eternity; far from it.

### 2. Heaven and earth are reunited only at the Cross
Atonement is the necessary ground of the New Creation. The most famous Old Testament prophecy of the New Creation is probably Isaiah 65 v 17-25, which begins, "See, I will create new heavens and a new earth..." But, strikingly, this New Creation centres and focuses on Jerusalem (v 18). In fact, it is impossible to separate the New Creation from the new Jerusalem. That is, in the imagery of Old Covenant language, heaven is reunited with earth through the place of atonement, the place of sacrifice. The logic is simple. Why was heaven estranged from earth? Because of sin, guilt and the wrath of God. So how can heaven be reunited with earth? Through atonement. It is for this reason that the crucified Lord is the only one in whom things in heaven and things on earth will be united (Ephesians 1 v 10). The cross of Christ is the intersection of earth and heaven. It is the place on earth where God's

space intersects with our space without destroying us utterly, because there the judgment fell on God.

### 3. The New Creation is ruled by Christ's people

In Romans 8 we read that creation "waits in eager expectation for the children of God to be revealed" and looks forward to being "brought into the freedom and glory of the children of God" (v 19, 21). But why is the future joy of creation so tied up with the children of God? The original purpose of God was for his good creation to be governed by a harmonious humanity. Creation is like a play in which the lead actors are drunk or absent, not playing their parts, or an orchestra in which the conductor is just having fun on his own behind the scenes. What creation needs is the sons and daughters of God, redeemed, restored, transformed, to govern it with justice. Then the orchestra will sing God's praises, and the play be performed to God's honour. This is the idea C.S. Lewis used when he spoke of Narnia waiting for "sons of Adam and daughters of Eve" to come and rule it. We do not yet see humankind governing the world as we ought, but we do see a human Jesus "crowned with glory and honour" and this means one day Christian people will "judge" (i.e. govern) the world (Hebrews 2 v 6-9; 1 Corinthians 6 v 2). The point Paul makes in 1 Corinthians 6 v 1-6 is that if we are going to govern the world in the age to come, we really ought to be able to learn to live together in harmony in this age, in the local church!

### 4. The New Creation is purged of all rebellion

For Babel to be finally reversed, the New Creation needs to be radically purged of all sin. The passage that perhaps stresses most forcibly the discontinuity between this age and the age to come is 2 Peter 3 v 3-13. Here we read that "the present heavens and earth are reserved for fire, being kept for the day of judgment and destruction of the ungodly" and "the heavens will disappear with a roar; the elements will be destroyed by fire, and the earth and everything done in it will be laid bare" (v 7, 10). The fires of judgment will have to burn very deep and will destroy, root and branch, all evildoers and sources of evil.

Even then, however, we must not misunderstand this as though Peter were simply teaching the replacement of this creation by an entirely discontinuous one. For Peter puts the fire of judgment in parallel with the waters of judgment in Noah's flood, under which the earth "was deluged and destroyed" (v 6). But the land then was not "destroyed" in an absolute sense: after the flood, the Bible story did not start again on Mars! No, the flood represented deep cleansing rather than simple replacement. Just so with the New Creation: the new heavens and earth are not a parallel universe, but this universe purged and redeemed.

We must not minimise the depth of this necessary purging. It is terribly possible to be "thrown into hell" or the "eternal fire" (Matthew 5 v 29-30; 18 v 8-9). There will be a terrible storm of judgment that will destroy every life not built on hearing Jesus' words and doing them (Matthew 7 v 24-27). There will be a deep and dreadful shaking and only the city with foundations will stand (Hebrews 12 v 26-28). It is possible finally to be excluded from the presence of the Lord, to be "thrown outside, into the darkness," to be consigned to eternal weeping and regrets (Matthew 8 v 12; 13 v 49-50). The sexually immoral, idolaters, adulterers, homosexual practitioners, thieves, the greedy, drunkards, revilers and swindlers will not inherit the kingdom of God (1 Corinthians 6 v 9-10). The cowardly, the unbelieving, the vile, murderers, the sexually immoral, sorcerers, idolaters and all liars will be thrown into the lake that burns with fire, which is the second death (Revelation 21 v 8). The New Creation cannot be born without terrible radical suffering and exclusion and so the form of this world as it is in this age, is passing away; it will be rolled up like unwanted clothes (1 Corinthians 7 v 31; Hebrews 1 v 11, quoting Psalm 102 v 26). Heaven and earth, in their rebellious corrupt form in this age, will pass away, as they did in the days of Noah: only Jesus' words and all that is built on that will last (Matthew 24 v 35).

## 5. Creation must be deeply transformed

This purging means the New Creation will be a deep transformation of this present age. I was preaching on this subject once and someone came up to me and asked, "How will there be room on this earth for all the believers who have ever lived? I can't visualise it." I think the New Testament gives us three answers to that sort of question.

1. Just as Jesus' resurrection body was real, physical and recognizable (the Jesus who rose was the same Jesus), and just as it was also transformed from weakness to glory, so the resurrection body will be deeply transformed, and the New Creation likewise will be deeply transformed.
2. When people asked Paul the same sort of question he said (in effect), *Don't ask stupid questions!* He wanted his questioners to grasp how deeply this body must be transformed to be suited to that new age, just as a seed is deeply transformed when it becomes its plant or crop. Our resurrection bodies will be so astonishingly greater they will be to these mortal bodies like plants to their seeds, like oak trees to acorns, or, as he puts it elsewhere, like a solid

building to a fragile tent (1 Corinthians 15 v 35-44; 2 Corinthians 5 v 1-5).

3. When the Sadducees tried to trick Jesus with this and came up with a clever conundrum, he replied, "You are in error because you do not know the Scriptures or the power of God" (Matthew 22 v 23-33).

So there's no point asking, "Where will London be? What about this planet? Will my dog be there?" These are foolish questions which reveal we have not grasped how deeply transformed the New Creation will be. It will be deeply and wonderfully transformed from the creation in this age. The New Creation will not be this creation trimmed with a few improved features added—as the pictures in the Jehovah's Witnesses magazines delivered to our doors suggest—a world that is pretty much recognizable as this world but with a few "tweaks" (perhaps a lion lying down with a lamb here or there!). The New Creation is unimaginably better, deeper, fuller, and more substantial, than this age. Every cell, every atom, and every molecule in the universe is corrupted and spoiled and not as it ought to be. The transformation necessary to root sin out of the universe is a root and branch matter.

So creation will be wonderfully and deeply transformed. We cannot achieve this by our human endeavours. No matter how well we do our politics, or measure up to our ecological responsibility (and we ought), we will never create the New Creation. It is the sovereign work of God alone and all the glory will be his.

In thinking about the New Creation, we need to be careful to give proper weight to the twin emphases in Scripture of continuity and discontinuity. If we go too far in the direction of continuity, we slip into a human-centred optimism which almost thinks by our actions we can turn this age into the age to come. We think of a world rather like this one but a bit better, such that by some good human initiatives, a bit of luck and a following wind we might create it ourselves. That would be nonsense. How arrogant!

On the other hand, if we go too far in the direction of discontinuity, we slip into thinking of the New Creation as a kind of "heaven" place which is a bit ghostly and insubstantial, and essentially a place that is entered by being taken out of this creation and beamed up by an interstellar teleporter like some kind of Christianized "Star Trekker" into a different place. If we think like this we will be inclined not to see the value of our secular work or our responsibilities to care for the environment and to seek justice in the world.

## Some Implications of the New Creation

The doctrine of the New Creation magnifies the church. It is a great antidote to western individualism, in which we regard the church as an aid to me in my discipleship, somewhere I go so that I may be encouraged. It is that (e.g. Hebrews 10 v 24-25), but it is much more. It is the anticipation in this age of the new humanity who will rule the age to come. It is the human society in which barriers are broken by the Cross, by justification through grace alone by faith alone; in which human pride is levelled, Babel undone, and men and women gathered in Christ to be all one in Christ Jesus, to be the united humanity that rules the age to come and inherits the earth. When we bring the New Creation to the front of the family photograph of Christian doctrines, we bring the doctrine of the church along with it.

This doctrine helps us think about Christian perseverance as a corporate thing. We are to endure to the end not only as individuals, but together. If we think that when we die we have arrived at our final destination, I fear we have removed from Christian discipleship a deep corporate incentive for perseverance. That is to say, I will hope for the future. I will long to be with Christ. But it will be "I" as an individual who longs, because when I die, my longings will be fulfilled, my path will be at an end.

However, it is interesting the New Testament does not seem to encourage this. When in James 5 the Christians are suffering because of injustice and poverty, James does not say, *Chin up, keep going: before long you will die and then it will all be alright for you (and let those who are still alive go hang).* No, he says, "Be patient, then, brothers and sisters, until the Lord's coming … be patient and stand firm, because the Lord's coming is near … The Judge is standing at the door!" (James 5 v 7-9). Keep waiting, keep on keeping on, hold on, because we are all together waiting in hope. We wait; the Christian dead wait and cry, "How long?"; the whole creation waits; even Christ himself waits for that great day. So let us hold on as we wait together and persevere together. This truth sets before believers a pattern for perseverance.

## Questions for Discussion

1. Review the chapter. What is God's plan for the end of time? How does this plan complete his glory?

2. In what ways will the New Creation be in continuity with this age, and in what ways will it be different?

3. What does the word "spiritual" in a phrase like "a spiritual body" mean in the New Testament, and how is this different from the popular use of the word "spiritual"?

4. I have suggested that talking about "heaven" can mislead us into forgetting the wonderful fullness of the New Creation. Do you think this is true? If so, how can we change the way we speak, to keep the New Creation in the centre of our thinking?

5. What difference does the doctrine of the New Creation make to the way we relate to other Christians?

6. When the local church seems very ordinary and sometimes discouraging, how can we help one another remember where it is heading?

# CONCLUSION

# The Glory of the God Who is One

We began our Bible tour with the God who is One. We will end with this same great God. At the start we glimpsed one harmonious creation that was the theatre of his glory. But very soon we saw that peace shattered in every way, in the tragic journey from Eden to Babel. The Bible story of the remaking of a broken world is not primarily about your or my individual salvation. Nor even is it primarily about our shared destiny as the children of God in the New Creation. Supremely it is about the restored glory of God. It is about the whole creation singing again his praises in harmony, with no discordant voices.

The New Creation will resound to the glory of God and of Christ. The New Creation will be—even more deeply than the unspoiled creation at the beginning—the theatre of God's glory. Creation will be restored and God will win: it will be a living visible tribute to his glory. Because atonement is its ground and foundation, the Lord Jesus Christ will stand at its centre as the Lamb who was slain. Because by his death the Son of God ransomed people for God, broke the barriers, and created a new united redeemed humanity, gathered from every nation, the glory will be to God alone.

Now he waits for all things to be put under his feet. The Bible story is about every hostile power surrendering to Jesus who will make them a footstool for his feet, and it is about this Jesus handing back the whole created order to the Father, "so that God may be all in all" (1 Corinthians 15 v 24-28). And when God is again all in all the song of the New Creation can begin in earnest, to be sung ever fresh for all eternity.

This is the destiny of the local church; this is the wonderful consummation for which the local church is preparing. The glory of God for all eternity is bound up with what happens in local churches now. They are the concrete realisation in this age of the peace-producing dynamics of the age to come. Let us commit ourselves to honouring God in the local church and praise God for every evidence we see in local churches that God is remaking a broken world. To him be the glory.

# Endnotes

1   Nick Spencer, *Beyond Belief? Barriers and Bridges to Faith Today* (The London Institute for Contemporary Christianity, 2003), p 17, 54.
2   Vaughan Roberts, *God's Big Picture* (IVP, 2002).
3   T. Desmond Alexander, *From Eden to the New Jerusalem* (IVP, 2008).
4   Gregory of Nazianzus, *Oration* 2, para.1 (362 AD).
5   Francis Schaeffer, *The God Who is There* (IVP, 1968).
6   *The Independent*, 12 April 1999.
7   The ESV is more literal here than the NIV.
8   *The Guardian*, 23 December 2006.
9   All quoted in Meic Pearse, *The Gods of War: Is Religion the Primary Cause of Violent Conflict?* (IVP, 2007), p 13, 14.
10  Isaiah 51 v 3; Joel 2 v 3; Ezekiel 28 v 13, 36 v 33-35.
11  *Nature* 365 (7 October 1993), p 484.
12  *The Calvin and Hobbes Tenth Anniversary Book* (Warner Books, 1995), p 184
13  John Steinbeck, *East of Eden* (first published 1952; my edition Penguin Classics, 2000), p 303-306, 602.
14  The King James Version translates the Hebrew imperfect tense very literally; but it is clear that it has the force of a command, as in the Ten Commandments ("Thou shalt...).
15  *The Economist*, 8 March 2008.
16  Eckhart Tolle, *A New Earth: Awakening to Your Life's Purpose* (Penguin, 2006), especially p 20-26, 57.
17  Genesis 3 v 15; 4 v 3-4, 15; 5 v 24; 7 v 13-16.
18  T. Desmond Alexander, *From Eden to New Jerusalem* (Kregel, 2009), p 30.

[19] *The Economist*, 14 March 2008, pp. 53, 56.

[20] Robert Cooper, *The Breaking of Nations: Order and Chaos in the Twenty-first Century* (Atlantic Monthly Press, 2003).

[21] Review in *The Economist*, 31 January 2009, p 63f.

[22] Quoted in Guy Brandon, *Just Sex: Is It Ever Just Sex?* (IVP, 2009), p 92.

[23] Jorge Luis Borges, *The Library of Babel* (David R. Godine, 2000).

[24] For this and many other fascinating uses of the Babel story in contemporary art, see I.L. Finkel and M.J. Seymour (eds) *Babylon: Myth and Reality* (The British Museum Press, 2008), p 203-208.

[25] Quoted in Allister Sparks, *The Mind of South Africa: The Story of the Rise and Fall of Apartheid* (Jonathan Ball publishers, 2003), p 294.

[26] Jonathan Sacks, *The Home We Build Together: Recreating Society* (Continuum, 2007), p 3.

[27] Otomo no Yakamochi.

[28] The closing date is written as 1918/19 because although the Armistice was signed in 1918 the Treaty of Versailles was not signed until 1919. It is interesting to note that a number of war memorials give 1914-19 as the dates.

[29] Quoted in Lesslie Newbigin, *The Light Has Come* (Eerdmans, 1982), p 160.

[30] Francis Fukuyama, *The End of History and the Last Man* (Penguin, 1993), p 233.

[31] Michael Jensen, "Fraternity", in *Churchman* 122/4, Winter 2008, p 331-334.

[32] Liam Goligher, *Joseph: The Hidden Hand of God* (Christian Focus, 2008), p 179.

[33] The KJV calls it "the church in the wilderness".

[34] See, e.g., Joshua 24, 1 Samuel 7 v 5-6 and Nehemiah 8.

[35] Edmund Gosse, *Father and Son* (Penguin, 1989), p 39.

[36] 1 Kings 19 v 12, translated "a gentle whisper" in NIV. No one knows the precise meaning of this word, and it certainly doesn't mean that we discern God's voice purely subjectively, as is sometimes suggested.

[37] C.S. Lewis, *A Grief Observed* (Faber, 1966), p 18, 19.

[38] Naomi Klein, *No Logo* (Knopf Canada, 2000), p 345.

[39] A fuller treatment of what follows is found in Alexander, *From Eden to the New Jerusalem* (as above), p 31-60.

[40] For example, 1 Chronicles 28 v 2 or Psalm 132 v 7 (another of the Psalms of Ascent).

[41] Alexander, *From Eden to the New Jerusalem* (as above), p 20-23.

[42] Genesis 3 v 8; Leviticus 26 v 12; Deuteronomy 23 v 14; 2 Samuel 7 v 6-7.

[43] Genesis 3 v 24; Exodus 25 v 18-22; 26 v 31; 36 v 8-38; 1 Kings 6 v 23-29; 2 Chronicles 3 v 14.

[44] Genesis 2 v 10; Ezekiel 47 v 1-12.

[45] Genesis 2 v 9; 3 v 22; Exodus 25 v 31-35.

[46] See also Psalm 22 v 25; 26 v 12; 35 v 18; 40 v 9-10.

[47] E.g. 1 Samuel 11 v 11; 28 v 4; 2 Samuel 10 v 17.

[48] E.g. Numbers 10 v 35; Psalm 68 v 1, 14, 30; 89 v 10; 92 v 9; 144 v 6; Isaiah 33 v 3; Jeremiah 49 v 32, 36; Nahum 3 v 18.

[49] 1 Samuel 16–2 Samuel 5. On this, see John Woodhouse's excellent study, *Looking for a Leader* (Crossway Books, 2008).

[50] 1 Kings 11 v 37-38; 12 v 26-33; 13 v 33-34.

[51] See also Ezekiel 12 v 12-14; 17 v 21; 22 v 15.

[52] See p 99 on Psalm 122 v 1-5.

[53] Kenneth Anger, *Hollywood Babylon* (Dell Publishing, 1975).

[54] C.S. Lewis, *The Great Divorce* (Collins, 1977), p 19.

[55] See the books of Ezra and Nehemiah. Also, e.g. Ezra 3 v 1; 7 v 28; 8 v 15; 9 v 4; 10 v 1; Nehemiah 5 v 16.

[56] One of the very best is John Stott, *The Cross of Christ* (IVP, 1986).

[57] Two recent helpful books are Graham Beynon, *God's New Community: New Testament Patterns for Today's Church* (IVP, 2005) and Melvin Tinker and Nathan Buttery, *Body Beautiful: Recovering the Biblical View of the Church* (Authentic Media, 2003).

[58] See Matthew 20 v 1-16, the parable of the labourers in the vineyard.

[59] *The Economist*, 18 October 2008, p 82.

[60] See also Matthew 26 v 3, 57; 27 v 62; Luke 22 v 66.

[61] The former, for example, in Lystra in Acts 14 v 19, or Thessalonica in Acts 17 v 5. The latter can be seen, for example, in Cyprus in

Acts 13 v 6-11, or in Ephesus in Acts 19 v 23-41.

[62] See also Matthew 10 v 32-33; 23 v 9.

[63] Tolle, *A New Earth* (as above), p 23.

[64] Paul Oakley, "Because of You" (Copyright © 1986 Thankyou Music).

[65] G.K. Beale, *The Book of Revelation* (Eerdmans, 1999), on Revelation 21 v 16.

# Index of
# Biblical References

**Genesis**

| | |
|---|---|
| Gen 1v1 | 28 |
| Gen 1v1–2v3 | 25 |
| Gen 1v26-28 | 25 |
| Gen 2v4-25 | 25-29 |
| Gen 2v8 | 25 |
| Gen 2v9 | 91 |
| Gen 2v10 | 91 |
| Gen 2v17 | 29,33 |
| Gen 3–10 | 30-37 |
| Gen 3v4 | 36,83 |
| Gen 3v5 | 29 |
| Gen 3v8 | 26, 30, 91 |
| Gen 3v13 | 30 |
| Gen 3v15 | 37 |
| Gen 3v22 | 44 |
| Gen 3v24 | 21, 91 |
| Gen 4v1-16 | 31-32 |
| Gen 4v3-4 | 37 |
| Gen 4v10 | 169 |
| Gen 4v15-19 | 75 |
| Gen 4v16 | 21 |
| Gen 4v18-24 | 32, 184 |
| Gen 5v24 | 37 |
| Gen 6v11 | 33 |

| | |
|---|---|
| Gen 7v13-16 | 37 |
| Gen 9v18-27 | 50 |
| Gen 10v5 | 72 |
| Gen 10v25 | 40 |
| Gen 11v1-9 | 39-45 |
| Gen 11v4 | 115 |
| Gen 11v5 | 67 |
| Gen 11v10 | 40 |
| Gen 11v10-32 | 61 |
| Gen 12–50 | 64 |
| Gen 12v1-3 | 62 |
| Gen 15v5 | 63 |
| Gen 17v4-8 | 63 |
| Gen 22v1-19 | 90 |
| Gen 22v17 | 63 |
| Gen 22v18 | 63 |
| Gen 28v3-4 | 63, 132 |
| Gen 28v10-22 | 90 |
| Gen 35v11 | 63, 132 |
| Gen 48v4 | 63, 132 |

**Exodus**

| | |
|---|---|
| Ex 1–15 | 65 |
| Ex 1v1-5 | 65 |
| Ex 1v6-7 | 65 |

| | |
|---|---|
| Ex 3v12 | 66 |
| Ex 6v7 | 12 |
| Ex 12v37-38 | 65 |
| Ex 13–18 | 65 |
| Ex 18v13-18 | 65 |
| Ex 19v20 | 67 |
| Ex 20v1-17 | 73 |
| Ex 20v12 | 74 |
| Ex 24v6-8 | 169 |
| Ex 25–40 | 90 |
| Ex 25v18-22 | 91 |
| Ex 25v31-35 | 91 |
| Ex 26v31 | 91 |
| Ex 32v1 | 75, 187 |
| Ex 36v8-38 | 91 |

**Leviticus**

| | |
|---|---|
| Lev 19v18 | 74 |
| Lev 23v4 | 89 |
| Lev 26v12 | 91 |

**Numbers**

| | |
|---|---|
| Num 10v11–36v13 | 87 |
| Num 10v35 | 97 |
| Num 16v11 | 190 |

**Deuteronomy**

| | |
|---|---|
| Deut 1v1 | 69 |
| Deut 1v9-12 | 66 |
| Deut 1v19–3v29 | 87 |
| Deut 4v10 | 67, 70 |
| Deut 4v10-15 | 71 |
| Deut 4v13 | 72 |
| Deut 4v14 | 72 |
| Deut 4v15-19 | 75 |
| Deut 4v20-24 | 80 |
| Deut 4v24 | 63 |
| Deut 4v25-27 | 111 |
| Deut 4v25-28 | 81 |
| Deut 4v30-31 | 84 |
| Deut 5v6-21 | 73 |
| Deut 6v4 | 11, 15 |
| Deut 9v10 | 68, 72 |
| Deut 10v4 | 68 |
| Deut 10v5 | 72 |
| Deut 18v16 | 68 |
| Deut 21v22-23 | 143 |
| Deut 23v2-4 | 68 |
| Deut 23v14 | 91 |
| Deut 28v15 | 111 |
| Deut 28v25 | 111 |
| Deut 28v64 | 111 |
| Deut 31v1 | 69 |
| Deut 31v11 | 69 |

**Joshua**

| | |
|---|---|
| Josh 13–21 | 95 |
| Josh 22 | 95 |
| Josh 24 | 68 |

**Judges**

| | |
|---|---|
| Jud 6v15 | 95 |
| Jud 8v1 | 95 |
| Jud 11v1 | 95 |
| Jud 12v1 | 95 |
| Jud 17–21 | 98 |
| Jud 20–21 | 95 |

**1 Samuel**

| | |
|---|---|
| 1 Sam 2v8 | 14 |

1 Sam 7v5-6        68
1 Sam 11v11        97
1 Sam 16v1-13      96
1 Sam 28v4         97

**2 Samuel**
2 Sam 5v6-9        88, 98
2 Sam 7v5-16       98
2 Sam 7v6-7        91
2 Sam 10v17        97

**1 Kings**
1 Kings 5–8        90
1 Kings 5v13-16    108
1 Kings 6v23-29    91
1 Kings 11v1-43    108
1 Kings 11v29-36   108-9
1 Kings 11v37-38   110
1 Kings 12         109
1 Kings 12v26-33   110
1 Kings 13v33-34   110
1 Kings 19v12      79

**2 Kings**
2 Kings 17v1-6     110
2 Kings 17v7-41    110
2 Kings 17v21      109
2 Kings 18–19      94
2 Kings 18–25      110
2 Kings 24,25

**1 Chronicles**
1 Chron 13v5       69
1 Chron 16v35      97
1 Chron 28v2       90

**2 Chronicles**
2 Chron 3v1        90
2 Chron 3v14       91
2 Chron 36v22-23   118

**Ezra**
Ezra 3v1           119
Ezra 7v28          119
Ezra 8v15          119
Ezra 9v4           119
Ezra 10v1          119

**Nehemiah**
Neh 1v8-9          118
Neh 5v16           119
Neh 8              68
Neh 8v1-8          119-120

**Esther**
Est 3v8            120-121

**Psalms**
Ps 2v2             190
Ps 22v25           96
Ps 26v12           96
Ps 35v18           96
Ps 40v9-10         96
Ps 44v11           112
Ps 47v2            15
Ps 47v9            63
Ps 48              93
Ps 50v5            67
Ps 68v1,14,30      97
Ps 68v26           96
Ps 84              91-92

| | |
|---|---|
| Ps 87 | 91 |
| Ps 89v10 | 97 |
| Ps 92v9 | 97 |
| Ps 102v26 | 213 |
| Ps 106v24-27 | 112 |
| Ps 106v47 | 121 |
| Ps 120 | 89,104 |
| Ps 121 | 89 |
| Ps 122 | 88-100, 120, 132 |
| Ps 125v1 | 93 |
| Ps 125v2 | 89 |
| Ps 132v7 | 90 |
| Ps 137 | 114-5, 116 |
| Ps 144v6 | 97 |

**Ecclesiastes**
| | |
|---|---|
| Eccles 5v2 | 16 |

**Isaiah**
| | |
|---|---|
| Is 1v13 | 188 |
| Is 2v1-4 | 100-101 |
| Is 5v7 | 99 |
| Is 10v13-14 | 51 |
| Is 11v12 | 122 |
| Is 13v1–14v23 | 115-116 |
| Is 13v11 | 115 |
| Is 14v4-6 | 115 |
| Is 14v13 | 115-116 |
| Is 27v12 | 122 |
| Is 33v3 | 97 |
| Is 40v11 | 122 |
| Is 43v5 | 122 |
| Is 47v8 | 116 |
| Is 49v5 | 122 |

| | |
|---|---|
| Is 51v3 | 26 |
| Is 52v13–53v12 | 141 |
| Is 53v6 | 46 |
| Is 56v8 | 122 |
| Is 60v4 | 122 |
| Is 65v17-25 | 210 |
| Is 66v18 | 122 |

**Jeremiah**
| | |
|---|---|
| Jer 9v13-16 | 112 |
| Jer 10v21 | 112 |
| Jer 13v24 | 112 |
| Jer 18v17 | 113 |
| Jer 23v1-2 | 113 |
| Jer 23v3 | 122 |
| Jer 29v14 | 122 |
| Jer 31v10 | 122 |
| Jer 3v10 | 122-3 |
| Jer 32v37 | 123 |
| Jer 49v32,36 | 97 |

**Lamentations**
| | |
|---|---|
| Lam 4v16 | 113 |

**Ezekiel**
| | |
|---|---|
| Ezek 11v16-17 | 123 |
| Ezek 12v12-14 | 113 |
| Ezek 17v21 | 113 |
| Ezek 20v23-24 | 113 |
| Ezek 22v15 | 113 |
| Ezek 28v13 | 26 |
| Ezek 28v25 | 123 |
| Ezek 34 | 136, 147-148 |
| Ezek 34v5-6 | 98, 148 |

| | | | |
|---|---|---|---|
| Ezek 34v12-13 | 123, 148 | Zeph 3v19-20 | 124 |
| Ezek 36v19,24 | 123 | | |
| Ezek 36v24-38 | 148 | **Haggai** | |
| Ezek 36v28 | 12 | Hag 1v1 | 121 |
| Ezek 36v33-35 | 26 | Hag 2v3 | 120 |
| Ezek 37v1-14 | 148-150 | | |
| Ezek 37v15-28 | 150-151 | **Zechariah** | |
| Ezek 37v21-22 | 123 | Zech 1v19 | 111 |
| Ezek 39v27-28 | 123 | Zech 7v13,14 | 113 |
| Ezek 47v1-12 | 91 | Zech 10v8-9 | 124 |
| | | Zech 14v9 | 15 |
| **Daniel** | | | |
| Dan 4v29-33 | 52 | **Matthew** | |
| | | Matt 1v1-17 | 133-4 |
| **Hosea** | | Matt 1v12 | 121 |
| Hos 1v1-9 | 110 | Matt 3v11 | 151-152 |
| Hos 1v10-11 | 124 | Matt 3v12 | 135 |
| Hos 2v14-23 | 124 | Matt 4v8 | 200 |
| | | Matt 4v18-22 | 135 |
| **Joel** | | Matt 4v23–5v1 | 135 |
| Joel 2v3 | 26 | Matt 5v5,12 | 204 |
| | | Matt 5v29-30 | 212 |
| **Amos** | | Matt 5v45,48 | 201 |
| Amos 5v21 | 188 | Matt 6v1-4 | 175-176, 201 |
| **Micah** | | Matt 6v10 | 16,201 |
| Mic 2v12 | 124 | Matt 6v20 | 203 |
| Mic 4v1-3 | 100-101 | Matt 6v32 | 201 |
| Mic 4v6 | 124 | Matt 7v24-27 | 212 |
| | | Matt 8v1-4 | 136 |
| **Nahum** | | Matt 8v10-12 | 140, 142, 143, 212 |
| Nah 3v18 | 97 | | |
| | | Matt 8v16-17 | 140 |
| **Zephaniah** | | Matt 9v9-11 | 136 |
| Zeph 3v10 | 124 | Matt 9v9-13 | 139 |

| | | | |
|---|---|---|---|
| Matt 9v35-38 | 136 | **Mark** | |
| Matt 9v36 | 98 | Mark 3v6 | 190 |
| Matt 10v32,33 | 191 | Mark 8v31 | 141 |
| Matt 10v34-39 | 138 | Mark 9v31 | 141 |
| Matt 11v19 | 136 | Mark 10v33-34 | 141 |
| Matt 12v6 | 102 | Mark 12v13 | 190 |
| Matt 12v30 | 137 | Mark 14v50 | 164 |
| Matt 12v32 | 206 | Mark 15v22 | 131 |
| Matt 13v40,49 | 206 | | |
| Matt 13v43 | 206 | **Luke** | |
| Matt 13v49-50 | 212 | Luke 1v51 | 45 |
| Matt 16v18 | 137, 171 | Luke 1v51-55 | 133 |
| Matt 18v1-4 | 171-173 | Luke 2v25-35 | 132-133 |
| Matt 18v4-6 | 174-175 | Luke 7v11-17 | 136 |
| Matt 18v8-9 | 212 | Luke 12v49-53 | 138 |
| Matt 18v15-20 | 182-3 | Luke 14v15-24 | 138 |
| Matt 18v21-35 | 182-185 | Luke 15v1 | 136 |
| Matt 19v21 | 203 | Luke 15v11-24 | 189 |
| Matt 19v28 | 207 | Luke 17v3-4 | 183-4 |
| Matt 20v1-16 | 185 | Luke 19v9 | 136 |
| Matt 21v31 | 176 | Luke 22v66 | 190 |
| Matt 22v1-14 | 138 | Luke 23v12 | 190 |
| Matt 22v23-33 | 214 | Luke 23v43 | 170 |
| Matt 22v30 | 210 | Luke 24v36-43 | 209 |
| Matt 23 | 176 | | |
| Matt 23v9 | 191 | **John** | |
| Matt 23v27-28 | 143 | John 1v11-13 | 157-158 |
| Matt 23v37 | 138 | John 1v14 | 102 |
| Matt 24v31 | 137 | John 1v29-34 | 151 |
| Matt 24v35 | 213 | John 1v46 | 173 |
| Matt 26v3,57 | 190 | John 2v19-22 | 103 |
| Matt 26v31 | 165 | John 3v1-8 | 158 |
| Matt 27v33 | 18 | John 7v37-39 | 152 |
| Matt 27v62 | 190 | John 7v41 | 173 |
| Matt 28v18 | 145, 201 | John 9v1-2 | 137 |

John 10v14-16    137
John 10v16       180
John 11v11       202
John 11v49-50    141
John 11v51-52    142
John 12v32       142, 165,
                 206
John 14v2        203
John 14v15-23    159-160
John 16v32       165
John 17v3        207
John 17v24       202
John 17v1-19     160
John 17v20-23    160
John 18v36       185, 206
John 20v17       201

**Acts**

Acts 1v4-5       153
Acts 1v12-26     153
Acts 2v1-13      61, 153-155
Acts 2v14-36     155
Acts 2v37-39     155
Acts 3v25        156
Acts 4v5-6       191
Acts 4v27        190
Acts 7v38        67, 166
Acts 8v1         165
Acts 11v19-21    165-166
Acts 11v20       177
Acts 13v6-11     191
Acts 14v19       191
Acts 17v5        191
Acts 19v23-41    191

**Romans**

Rom 1v5          145
Rom 1v23-25      78
Rom 3v21-27      171
Rom 4v13         64, 153
Rom 5v1          144
Rom 5v1-11       170
Rom 5v10-11      144
Rom 5v12         34
Rom 8v18-22      209, 211
Rom 12v21        185-186
Rom 16v26        145

**1 Corinthians**

1 Cor 1v1-2      179-180
1 Cor 3v9,16     167
1 Cor 3v16       103
1 Cor 5v4        166
1 Cor 6v1-6      211
1 Cor 6v9-10     212
1 Cor 6v19       103
1 Cor 7v31       213
1 Cor 8v4        12
1 Cor 8v6        12
1 Cor 12v4-6     156
1 Cor 14v33      157
1 Cor 15v24-28   220
1 Cor 15v35-44   213
1 Cor 15v44      209

**2 Corinthians**

2 Cor 1v20       134
2 Cor 5v1-5      213
2 Cor 5v21       144
2 Cor 6v16       103

**Galatians**
Gal 2v11-16    178
Gal 3v8    62
Gal 3v13    144, 152
Gal 3v13-14    152-153
Gal 3v16    62
Gal 3v29    62
Gal 4v25    102
Gal 4v26    207

**Ephesians**
Eph 1v3    203
Eph 1v9-10    197, 210
Eph 1v11-14    203
Eph 1v21    206
Eph 2v6    203
Eph 2v14-18    177
Eph 2v21-22    103
Eph 4v3-6    157
Eph 4v12-13    157
Eph 4v28    74
Eph 5v5    78
Eph 6v2-3    74
Eph 6v12    201

**Philippians**
Phil 1v6    204
Phil 1v23    202-203
Phil 2v6-11    145
Phil 2v8    173
Phil 3v11    204
Phil 3v20-21    203, 204

**Colossians**
Col 3v5    78

Col 3v12-13    182

**1 Thessalonians**
1 Thess 2v14    180
1 Thess 4v13    202

**2 Thessalonians**
2 Thess 1v7
2 Thess 2v1    208

**1 Timothy**
1 Tim 6v17    74

**2 Timothy**
2 Tim 3v5    188

**Hebrews**
Heb 1v11    213
Heb 2v5    206
Heb 2v6-9    211
Heb 6v5    206
Heb 9v24    201
Heb 10v12-13    201, 206
Heb 10v24-25    167, 215
Heb 11v28    169
Heb 12v18    84, 168
Heb 12v18-21    83, 168
Heb 12v18-29    167
Heb 12v22    87, 101, 103, 168, 207
Heb 12v22-24    168-9
Heb 12v25    168
Heb 12v26-28    212
Heb 12v29    83, 168
Heb 13v5    74, 181

**James**

| | |
|---|---|
| James 2v2 | 166 |
| James 2v13 | 184 |
| James 4v1-3 | 180-181 |
| James 4v4-10 | 181 |
| James 5v7-9 | 216 |

**1 Peter**

| | |
|---|---|
| 1 Pet 1v4 | 203, 204 |
| 1 Pet 2v11 | 203 |
| 1 Pet 2v5 | 103, 167 |
| 1 Pet 2v23 | 186 |
| 1 Pet 3v18 | 169 |
| 1 Pet 3v22 | 201 |
| 1 Pet 5v9 | 180 |

**2 Peter**

| | |
|---|---|
| 2 Pet 3v3-13 | 211-212 |

**1 John**

| | |
|---|---|
| 1 John 5v21 | 78 |

**Revelation**

| | |
|---|---|
| Rev 6v10 | 205 |
| Rev 7v9 | 63, 207 |
| Rev 21v2 | 103 |
| Rev 21v2,10 | 208 |
| Rev 21v5 | 209 |
| Rev 21v8 | 212 |
| Rev 21v25 | 208 |

# Acknowledgements

I am grateful to The Good Book Company for bringing this Bible overview back into print, some years after its original publication by Authentic Media. Many years ago I did a personal Bible study on the themes of "scattering" and "gathering"; it proved such a fruitful exploration that eventually it developed into this fuller study. I am grateful for many helpful comments from my wife Carolyn, my friend Jason Fletcher, my former colleagues Tim McMahon, Stuart Allen, Christine Mulryne and Nikki Tomkins at the Cornhill Training Course, and to Zoë Moore and Katy Morgan for their editing of the original and now the reissued version.

# thegoodbook
## COMPANY

**BIBLICAL | RELEVANT | ACCESSIBLE**

At The Good Book Company, we are dedicated to helping Christians and local churches grow. We believe that God's growth process always starts with hearing clearly what he has said to us through his timeless word—the Bible.

Ever since we opened our doors in 1991, we have been striving to produce Bible-based resources that bring glory to God. We have grown to become an international provider of user-friendly resources to the Christian community, with believers of all backgrounds and denominations using our books, Bible studies, devotionals, evangelistic resources, and DVD-based courses.

We want to equip ordinary Christians to live for Christ day by day, and churches to grow in their knowledge of God, their love for one another, and the effectiveness of their outreach.

Call us for a discussion of your needs or visit one of our local websites for more information on the resources and services we provide.

Your friends at The Good Book Company

thegoodbook.com | thegoodbook.co.uk
thegoodbook.com.au | thegoodbook.co.nz
thegoodbook.co.in